JOHN NICHOLSON

John Nicholson is a writer, performer and director, and is an Artistic
Director of the award-winning Peepolykus, with whom he has created
twelve productions that have toured the company worldwide and into the
West End with *The Hound of the Baskervilles* (West Yorkshire
Playhouse). This comic adaptation, co-written with Steven Canny, has
been licensed all over the world, with over one hundred productions to
date. This, alongside *The Massive Tragedy of Madame Bovary*
(co-written with Javier Marzan), *Dracula: The Bloody Truth* and *The
Three Musketeers* (both co-written with La Navet Bete), is published by
Nick Hern Books. Further writing/directing credits include *Shaun the
Sheep Live* (Aardman); *No Wise Men* (Liverpool Playhouse/Bristol Old
Vic); *Dick Tracy, A Christmas Carol, Aladdin* (Le Navet Bete); *Paul
Merton – My Obsession* (Edinburgh); *Spyski – The Importance of Being
Honest* (Lyric Hammersmith); *The Arthur Conan Doyle Appreciation
Society* (Traverse Theatre, Edinburgh); *Richard III's Rampage* (Old Vic/
world tour); Nina Conti in *Dolly Mixtures* (Sydney Opera House, West
End); Mike McShane in *Mon Droit* (Edinburgh); *Paul Merton – Out of
His Head* (Vaudeville Theatre, West End); *Origins* (Pentabus);
Spymonkey's Spookshow (Blackpool Winter Gardens); comedy
consultancy on *A Little Hotel on the Side* (Bath Theatre Royal).
Writing commissions for radio include *Marley was Dead, Baskervilles,
A Trespasser's Guide to the Classics* (Series 1 and 2), *Rik Mayall's
Bedside Tales* (BBC Radio 4). Writing commissions for television
include *Under Surveillance, Comedy Nation* (BBC 3); *A Salted Nut*
(Paramount); *The Mulligans, Off Their Rockers* (ITV). Forthcoming
theatre adaptations include *The Time Machine* and *Treasure Island*.

T0353247

LE NAVET BETE

Le Navet Bete is a physical-comedy theatre company based in Exeter, Devon, whose spectacular and hilarious shows have wowed audiences globally since their formation in 2007. The company of five (Al Dunn, Matt Freeman, Dan Bianchi, Nick Bunt and Alex Best) first met each other whilst studying on the Theatre and Performance course at the University of Plymouth in 2003 and, since graduating, have produced fourteen indoor and three outdoor performances to huge critical acclaim and success. Their first two shows *Serendipity* and *Zemblanity*, heavily influenced by bouffon and non-narrative structures, were performed at the Edinburgh Festival Fringe in 2008 and 2009 respectively and gained multiple five-star reviews. As the company developed and grew over the following years, their inimitable style of performance became much more storytelling/narrative-driven with hit shows such as *A Christmas Carol*, *Dick Tracy*, *Dracula: The Bloody Truth* and *Aladdin* placing physical theatre, fooling and slapstick at the heart of it. With Exeter as their base, they are Associate Artists at the Exeter Northcott Theatre, where *The Three Musketeers: A Comedy Adventure* premiered in 2019. The company are also Artists in Residence at the Exeter Phoenix and are co-producing partners with the Barbican Theatre, Plymouth, to deliver their annual Christmas show to sell-out audiences every year. Making accessible work has been at the centre of Le Navet Bete's ethos right from the very beginning. This saw them diversify into outdoor performance in 2010, quickly becoming one of the UK's most ridiculously outrageous, much-loved outdoor acts. They have since performed thousands of outdoor shows from the circus fields at Glastonbury Festival, and the beautiful gardens of the Herrenhausen Palace in Hanover, Germany, to the picturesque Plaza de Armas in Morelia, Mexico, and high up on the side of the Rock of Gibraltar. As well as performing, the company have a widely renowned education programme specialising in clowning, physical comedy, performer–audience relationships and play, that they have taught in schools, colleges and universities across the world from the Royal Central School of Speech and Drama in London to the Universidad Nacional Autonoma de Mexico in Mexico City. *The Three Musketeers: A Comedy Adventure* is Le Navet Bete's sixth collaboration with John Nicholson at the directing helm and the first time working alongside Lea Anderson MBE as movement and co-director.

John Nicholson & Le Navet Bete

THE THREE MUSKETEERS

A Comedy Adventure

*Adapted from the novel
by Alexandre Dumas*

NICK HERN BOOKS

London

www.nickhernbooks.co.uk

A Nick Hern Book

The Three Musketeers first published in Great Britain in 2019 as a paperback original by Nick Hern Books Limited, The Glasshouse, 49a Goldhawk Road, London W12 8QP, in association with Le Navet Bete

The Three Musketeers copyright © 2019 John Nicholson and Le Navet Bete

John Nicholson and Le Navet Bete have asserted their moral right to be identified as the authors of this work

Cover image: Graphic Design by Dave Robertson and Rebecca Pitt; Images by Matt Austin

Designed and typeset by Nick Hern Books, London
Printed in the UK by Mimeo Ltd, Huntingdon, Cambridgeshire PE29 6XX

A CIP catalogue record for this book is available from the British Library

ISBN 978 1 84842 869 0

Woodland
CARBON
www.woodlandcarbon.co.uk
NICK HERN BOOKS
Printed on Carbon Captured paper

Author's Note

This play began life with a two-week devising process with the British theatre company Le Navet Bete. Following design discussions with Ti Green, which embraced and developed the 'halcyon days' concept/framing device, I wrote a first draft in January 2019. Sasha Yevtushenko, a radio producer who has edited a number of plays I've written for the BBC, encouraged me to look more keenly at how the adaptation would land with a contemporary audience. Further drafts followed in response to input from Le Navet Bete before and during rehearsals. The version you're holding is the tenth draft.

Mention *The Three Musketeers* to anyone and naturally there is an expectation of sword-fighting. I wanted to capture the energy of sword-fighting through the physicality of the performance and pace of the unfolding narrative, with split images and scene/costume changes transitioning over one another. Our approach to the sword-fighting itself was to reflect on how children fought with wooden swords. We were also inspired by Apache dance for conflict scenes.

On the whole, productions of Dumas' epic are produced with large casts. They often concentrate on the first half of the book and compress the second. We wanted to embrace the novel in its entirety because we felt it allows for the arc of relationships to play out. It also exposes flaws in the characters that we wanted to play with. In terms of overall feel, we wanted to draw on the 'escapist' flavour of the book; the sense of play, the reason why *The Three Musketeers* has a reputation for being larky (despite some pretty dark themes lurking beneath the surface). Lastly, we wanted to have fun with the characters, but particularly with Milady de Winter. She is one of literature's most intriguing femme fatales and, in my view, shouldn't be upstaged by the musketeers (who are on the whole more reactive than proactive in the original). Although we've used plot points as launchpads for comedy, we were keen to remain faithful to the events of the

original novel. I hope you enjoy reading it. If you are
considering performing this play, the composed music for the
original production is available for licensing too.

John Nicholson

This stage adaptation of *The Three Musketeers* was first performed by Le Navet Bete at The Exeter Northcott on 1 May 2019. The cast was as follows:

ACTORS	Al Dunn
	Dan Bianchi
	Matt Freeman
	Nick Bunt
Adapter and Director	John Nicholson
Movement and Co-Director	Lea Anderson MBE
Set Designer	Ti Green
Costume Designer	Fi Russell
Composer	Peter Coyte
Lighting Designer	Marcus Bartlett
Script Editor	Sasha Yevtushenko
Production and Technical Manager	Alex 'Wheaty' Best
Stage Manager	Abi Cowan
Scenic Painter	James Andrews
Set Builder	Steel Monkey Engineering
Canvas Maker	Spencer Rouse
Marketing and Audience Development Manager	Anna Bunt
Photoshoot Costume Designer	Sarah Dicks
Promotional Image Photographer	Matt Austin
Trailer Location Photographer	Artur Tixiliski
Production Photographer	Mark Dawson
Videographer	Simon's Kitchen
Graphic Design	Dave Robertson
Additional Graphic Design	Rebecca Pitt Creative

Characters

ACTOR 1, *Al*
ACTOR 2, *Dan*
ACTOR 3, *Becky*
ACTOR 4, *Emma*
D'ARTAGNAN
MAMAN
PAPA
DOG
TRAVERS
BARMAN/BAR LADY
BLACKSMITH
MILADY
CARDINAL RICHELIEU
CAPTAIN TREVILLE
ARAMIS
ATHOS
PORTHOS
CARDINAL GUARD 1
CARDINAL GUARD 2
CARDINAL GUARD 3
CARDINAL GUARD 4
MONSIEUR BONACIEUX
CONSTANCE
LORD BUCKINGHAM
QUEEN ANNE
LOUVRE GUARD
COURTIER
KING LOUIS
MESSENGER
BUCKINGHAM'S FRIEND
    TORQUIL
JEWELLER
KITTY
COMTE DE WARDES

PUB LANDLORD
FELTON
BUCKINGHAM'S FRIEND
    BERTIE
SISTER MARY
PRAYING NUN

Note on Play

The play is written for four actors, two women and two men, with doubling. The actors play versions of themselves when they talk directly to the audience, or when they're 'outside of the play'. Future productions should adjust the names of the actors accordingly. References to contemporary locations such as the theatre the play is being performed in, length of run, ticket prices, etc., may be adjusted accordingly.

The advised casting works as follows:

ACTOR 1 (*Al*), D'Artagnan, Cardinal Guard 1, Praying Nun, Courtier, Buckingham's friend Bertie, Comte de Wardes (once real)

ACTOR 2 (*Dan*), Athos, Blacksmith, King Louis, Monsieur Bonacieux, Lord Buckingham, Kitty, Papa, Captain Treville, Cardinal Guard 2, Sister Mary, Messenger

ACTOR 3 (*Becky*), Porthos, Milady, Queen Anne, Maman, Cardinal Guard 3

ACTOR 4 (*Emma*), Aramis, Cardinal Richelieu, Constance, Felton, Barman/Bar Lady, Travers, Cardinal Guard 4, Louvre Guard, Buckingham's friend Torquil, Jeweller, Comte de Wardes (once real, once disguised), Pub Landlord

The set consists of playing areas at three different levels. The lowest is table height and is on wheels.

The further up the structure we go, leaves and branches turn into gold-plated rococo moulding. At the top, it's palatial. At ground level, it's den-like. Costumes (for character changes) are hung on the set.

This text went to press before the end of rehearsals and so may differ slightly from the play as performed.

ACT ONE

Scene One

Birdsong plays as the audience take their seats. BECKY *and* EMMA *appear in spots on middle and top levels and duet together.*

BECKY *and* EMMA.
Welcome to this tale from France
Of gallantry and great romance
Of honour, valour, trust and sometimes tears
This story of four musketeers.

Lights up on the den below, where DAN *is checking his watch and* AL *is fixing his bike.*

BECKY. How did that sound?

DAN (*simultaneous*). Awful.

AL (*simultaneous*). Rubbish.

EMMA. Oh, thanks a lot.

DAN. That's time. Calling all musketeers to attention. Athos? All for one. D'Artagnan?

AL. All for one.

DAN. Aramis?

EMMA. What?

DAN. All for one. And Porthos?

BECKY. Can't we just say 'Here'?

DAN *and* AL. No.

DAN. Item one. Evidence of trespass in the musketeers' headquarters. Who are we putting on the suspects list?

AL. What about the Smith twins?

DAN. Or Mitchell Thompson.

BECKY. Or a badger?

AL. A badger?

DAN. You think a badger can unscrew a bottle of Fanta and pour himself a cup, do you?

BECKY. Yeah.

DAN. This isn't *Wind in the Willows*. Musketeers, I suggest we split up and look for evidence.

BECKY. Okay, wait, hang on. It was me.

DAN. You!?

BECKY. Me and Emma came here yesterday after school.

DAN. And had some Fanta?

BECKY. Yes.

DAN. And didn't write it down in the book?

BECKY. I forgot.

AL. You have to write it down!

BECKY. Alright, keep your hair on, Al.

AL. D'Artagnan!

DAN. And scene.

Everyone drops out of character.

Scene Two

DAN. Ladies and gentlemen, we'll explain what all that was about in just a moment. But firstly, welcome to the Theatre Royal and to this theatrical adaptation of the most widely read book in the world.

BECKY. – apart from the Bible.

EMMA. – most widely read *French* book.

DAN. To the most widely read *French* book –

BECKY. – novel.

DAN. To the most widely read French novel in the world, apart from the Bible.

BECKY. – which isn't a novel.

EMMA. – or French.

DAN. Welcome to *The Three Musketeers*!

AL. Now, what we want to explain first is that Becky, Emma, Dan and I have all known each other since junior school. And when we were about nine or ten...

DAN. I was eleven – that's why I was put in charge.

AL. But you're not now.

DAN. Sort of still am.

AL. When we were younger, we formed a gang – basically because we were obsessed with *The Three Musketeers*.

BECKY. Well, mainly you and Dan were. Emma and I just wanted to be in a gang.

AL. And then we carried on being friends through high school...

EMMA. Although some of us went to different schools.

AL. Yeah, and eventually we all ended up on the same performing arts course and started making touring theatre shows together /

DAN. And now we're here; at the Theatre Royal for four nights. Awesome!

BECKY. So about a year ago we had to think of a new title to adapt and one of us said /

DAN. It was me.

BECKY. What about *The Three Musketeers*?

AL. Sort of a no-brainer. And so we've recreated our den, with the treehouse and all the costumes and... well pretty much everything really.

BECKY. Well *we* didn't, we had an incredible creative team: (*Lists creatives working on the production.*)

EMMA. Not forgetting Abi our stage manager there, who's amazing – you'll see.

The SM *is visible throughout the show assisting with costume changes, props, etc.*

AL. So, back in the day we obviously cast ourselves as the four musketeers /

DAN. I was Athos because I was the oldest. Becky was Porthos, Emma was Aramis and Al was D'Artagnan.

AL. Most handsome.

DAN. That's right – cos he was the youngest.

EMMA. And as well as playing the four musketeers, we'll also be playing every other significant character from the original text.

DAN. How? One word – acting talent.

EMMA. That's two words.

DAN. Multi-character work.

EMMA. Three words.

DAN. Super-quick-change costumes. Five.

BECKY. Four. Between us we shall play more than thirty characters, with just the occasional help from you the audience. But don't be alarmed by that.

AL. Well, maybe a bit, but I'm mainly looking at you, madame.

DAN. So, without further ado…

EMMA. Sweets!

AL. No, we said no to sweets, this isn't a kids' show.

EMMA. Oh come on, who doesn't like something to suck!?

She throws sweets into the audience and ad libs.

DAN. Ladies and gentlemen, the year is 1606 and a very special baby has just been born.

BECKY. A baby boy, called –

EMMA (*simultaneous*). Jesus.

AL (*simultaneous*). D'Artagnan!

EMMA. I meant D'Artagnan.

> *Music begins.* DAN *and* BECKY *get changed into* PAPA
> *and* MAMAN *respectively.* AL *helps operate*
> D'ARTAGNAN *puppets.* EMMA *becomes a* DOG.

Scene Three

A montage of D'ARTAGNAN *growing up, telling the following story:*

Proud parents holding a baby.

Photo 1: baby puppet.

MAMAN *tries to deal with crying baby while* PAPA *chops wood.*

MAMAN *despairs of* D'ARTAGNAN*'s crying, so* MAMAN *and* PAPA *swap roles.*

MAMAN *chops wood while* PAPA *tries to get* D'ARTAGNAN *to hold a sword (as a baby). He drops it twice but then holds it and stabs* PAPA *in the balls.*

MAMAN *tries to feed* D'ARTAGNAN *but he swipes the bowl into the air with the sword.* MAMAN *pulls sword away from him.*

Photo 2: they then turn and the baby puppet is replaced with toddler puppet.

Photo 3: D'ARTAGNAN *stabs parents in the knees and is sent to play on his own while* MAMAN *and* PAPA *work on farm.*

MAMAN *and* PAPA *sadly watch* D'ARTAGNAN *play on his own.* MAMAN *whistles and a* DOG (EMMA) *enters.* D'ARTAGNAN *is very happy and rides the* DOG *like a horse and sword-fights* PAPA.

Transition where puppet is replaced by AL *riding the* DOG.
He beats PAPA *in the sword fight. They hug. Family photo with*
DOG. *The group disperses.*

D'ARTAGNAN *starts to pack a bag. The* DOG *watches him,
then stands up to sing...*

EMMA.
Long long ago, somewhere in France
A boy prepares to say farewell
To his parents and to his home
To the only life he's ever known.

EMMA *returns to all-fours and follows* D'ARTAGNAN *off.*

Scene Four

PAPA *stares out, trying to hold it together.* MAMAN *enters.*

PAPA. Is he all packed?

MAMAN. Yes.

PAPA. What's he doing?

MAMAN. Saying goodbye to Droolius Caesar.

PAPA. God, that dog's gonna miss him.

EMMA *whimpers (off).* PAPA *is now really struggling
to hold back the tears.*

MAMAN. No. Don't you go, you'll set me off again.

PAPA. I'm not going.

MAMAN. Your lip's wibbling.

PAPA. No it isn't.

D'ARTAGNAN *enters, finishing packing his bag.*

D'ARTAGNAN. Right then.

MAMAN. Here, I've made you up some special wound-healing ointment.

D'ARTAGNAN. Maman.

MAMAN. And I packed you a clean hanky too.

D'ARTAGNAN. Maman, please, you're embarrassing us both! I'm a man now.

PAPA. That's right, Jill. He's a man now. And a remarkably talented swordsman too.

MAMAN. You remember to write to us.

D'ARTAGNAN. Like I said, Jill – if time permits. But it's likely I'll be much in demand. And incredibly popular with the ladies too.

PAPA. That's my boy! Now, here's your letter of recommendation to Monsieur Treville – the Captain of the King's musketeers in Paris – a kind, fair and generous old friend of mine.

D'ARTAGNAN. I'll fight him if I have to.

PAPA. No, don't fight him, you're just asking him for a job!

D'ARTAGNAN. Let's just hope he makes the right decision then.

MAMAN. Now, D'Artagnan, you mustn't get hot-headed.

D'ARTAGNAN. Maman, please! I'm a man now!

PAPA. Son, I want you to take Leon Trotsky.

D'ARTAGNAN. Papa, no. You need him to pull the plough.

PAPA. You can't arrive in Paris without a horse. Lead him in, Travers.

TRAVERS (*Irish*) *wheels in an old Chopper bike but handles it like a bucking horse.*

Travers, for goodness' sake, calm him down!

TRAVERS. I'm doing my best, sir, but he's awful spooked.

PAPA. Get a proper grip on him, man!

Horse calms.

D'ARTAGNAN. But he's so old, Papa. Will he even reach Paris?

PAPA. He'll still be useful even if he doesn't.

D'ARTAGNAN. How?

PAPA. You can hollow him out and sleep in him.

Horse neighs and bucks.

Travers! (*Shouts at* TRAVERS *unintelligibly.*)

TRAVERS. But, sir… (*Protests unintelligibly, ending with:*) Fecking horse.

PAPA. Just hold him steady while I saddle him up. Come on, boy, easy.

PAPA fits a bike saddle.

And remember what I've taught you; never submit to insults – except from the King – and when you find yourself with your back against the wall /

D'ARTAGNAN. Turn round and march forward!

PAPA. Um. Not quite.

MAMAN. You'll give yourself a nose bleed if you do that.

D'ARTAGNAN. Maman, please! I must get going.

He swings his leg onto the bike but manages to boot TRAVERS *in the face.*

You've both made a good stab at raising me, but I'll take it from here. À bientôt! Yah!

He cycles off.

MAMAN. My darling boy.

As they watch him leave, MAMAN *hugs an awkward* PAPA. TRAVERS *then goes in for a hug.*

PAPA. Travers, what are you doing!?

TRAVERS. Sorry, sir, I thought it was a group hug.

PAPA. Get back to work!

> D'ARTAGNAN *rides through France as* EMMA *changes into* BARMAN *and* DAN *into* BLACKSMITH, *all in view of the audience.*

Scene Five

D'ARTAGNAN *parks his bike, gives it a nosebag, then enters a sleepy bar.*

D'ARTAGNAN. What have you got on draught, my good man?

BARMAN. Are you over eighteen?

D'ARTAGNAN. Yeah, like way over!

BARMAN. We only sell absinthe and pastis.

D'ARTAGNAN. Very well, a pint of absinthe and one pasty – steak and kidney if you've got it. I also need a room for the night. Any single women in town?

BARMAN. One or two.

D'ARTAGNAN. Better make it a double then.

BARMAN. I'll see what I've got.

> BARMAN *exits. A* BLACKSMITH *laughs at* D'ARTAGNAN*'s horse then enters the bar.*

BLACKSMITH.That your horse outside?

D'ARTAGNAN. What of it?

> BLACKSMITH *chuckles again.*

You might not find my horse so amusing if I were to challenge you to a duel!

> *The* BLACKSMITH *grabs him by the balls.*

BLACKSMITH. I think what you meant to say was, 'Please, lovely Mr Blacksmith man, could you reshoe my nancy buttercup-coloured old nag.'

D'ARTAGNAN (*scared and in pain*). Please, Mr Buttercup man, could you /

BLACKSMITH. Course I can. Two francs.

D'ARTAGNAN. Two francs!? (*Sound effect: balls crunching.*) No okay, fair enough.

The BLACKSMITH *exits and* D'ARTAGNAN *hobbles back to the bar.* MILADY *enters from upstairs. She's beautiful and devilishly stylish.* D'ARTAGNAN *watches her as she buys cigarettes from a machine.*

She places a cigarette in her mouth. D'ARTAGNAN *strikes a match which goes out. She uses a lighter.*

Gauloises. Nice. So, what brings a beautiful lady like you to a bar like this?

MILADY. Clearly the prospect of meeting a teenager like you.

BAR LADY *enters.*

BAR LADY. A sealed message arrived for you while you were out, madame. One moment. (*Exits.*)

D'ARTAGNAN. I leave for Paris in the morning and the night is still young.

BARMAN *enters with key for* D'ARTAGNAN.

BARMAN. Room nine, mate – top of the stairs.

D'ARTAGNAN. You mean my... *double* room.

BARMAN. Twin. All I've got left.

D'ARTAGNAN. No problem. I'll push the beds together.

BARMAN. It's a bunk bed.

D'ARTAGNAN. Has anyone ever told you your eyes resemble the rich blue of alpine lakes?

BARMAN. No.

D'ARTAGNAN. Not you. I insist you let me buy you a drink.

MILADY. Dom Pérignon.

BARMAN. D'accord.

BARMAN exits.

D'ARTAGNAN. You're obviously not from around here.

MILADY. No. I have a château in the Loire Valley.

D'ARTAGNAN. A whole… château. Right. And what do you do for kicks?

BARMAN enters with bottle.

MILADY. Kill people.

Champagne cork flies out.

D'ARTAGNAN. Ha! I like a woman with a sense of humour. I expect you're wondering what my business is in Paris.

MILADY. No.

D'ARTAGNAN. I'm about to become a King's musketeer.

MILADY smirks.

You doubt me? I have a letter of introduction.

*He searches his bag. MILADY poisons his drink.
D'ARTAGNAN shows her the letter.*

MILADY. Golly. Well you must be very brave and strong.

D'ARTAGNAN. I'm just an incredibly gifted swordsman.

BAR LADY enters.

BAR LADY. Your message, madame.

*MILADY reads the message. D'ARTAGNAN takes a gulp
of his drink.*

D'ARTAGNAN. Why don't we take these upstairs? Barman, lady, stick the bubbles on ice and send them up to my room.

BAR LADY exits with bottle.

MILADY. You're very sure of yourself, aren't you…

D'ARTAGNAN. D'Artagnan. Let's just say I hate to miss out on an opportunity.

MILADY. Me too.

D'ARTAGNAN. And you are?

MILADY. About to rob you.

D'ARTAGNAN starts to choke. MILADY calmly steals his money and takes the letter from his hand as he falls to the floor. BAR LADY returns with champagne on ice.

Change of plan. I won't be staying tonight after all. I must head to Paris.

BAR LADY. And the gentleman?

MILADY. I think the absinthe must have gone to his head. If he doesn't puke he'll probably die.

MILADY exits. The BAR LADY runs around the bar to help D'ARTAGNAN, who pukes as she pulls him up.

BAR LADY. Come on, you. You can sleep it off upstairs.

She drags D'ARTAGNAN off, then the same actor changes into CARDINAL RICHELIEU. MILADY crosses the set and then hides in the shadows. A sign held by the SM reads 'Cardinal Richelieu's, Paris'.

Scene Six

Sound effect: Gregorian chanting.

CARDINAL RICHELIEU. Now is the winter of our discontent made glorious summer by… well, me quite frankly. Ha! I will set the King of France and his Queen in deadly hate, the one against the other.

MILADY steps out of the shadows.

MILADY. Cardinal Richelieu. Plagiarising Shakespeare again?

CARDINAL RICHELIEU. You're late.

MILADY. You're fat. What do you want?

CARDINAL RICHELIEU. I've told you before not to smoke in my vestry.

She lights a cigarette.

I have another little assignment. Sit down.

MILADY. No.

CARDINAL RICHELIEU. Sit down!

MILADY. No.

CARDINAL RICHELIEU. Fine. Stand then.

She sits.

It has come to my attention that Queen Anne /

MILADY. Who?

CARDINAL RICHELIEU. The Queen of France!

MILADY. Are you referring to the woman who rejected your sexual advances?

CARDINAL RICHELIEU. How dare you.

MILADY. How dare *you*. It must drive you mad that she's also an immigrant.

CARDINAL RICHELIEU. You are aware I could have you killed.

MILADY. And you are aware I could kill you… myself. You were saying?

CARDINAL RICHELIEU. I have reason to believe that Queen Anne is conducting 'liaisons' with the British Prime Minister, Lord Buckingham.

MILADY. No, really? Keep up, Grandpa.

CARDINAL RICHELIEU. How could you possibly have already known that?

MILADY. Your low estimation of me is actually *really* concerning!

CARDINAL RICHELIEU. Listen! There's a letter on its way to him from her.

MILADY. Which you want intercepted?

CARDINAL RICHELIEU. Exactly.

MILADY. So you can expose their affair to King Louis?

CARDINAL RICHELIEU. That's my business.

MILADY. And all because you can't handle the fact that the Queen has more influence over the King than you.

CARDINAL RICHELIEU. You really do test my patience, Ursula.

MILADY. Ursula?

CARDINAL RICHELIEU. Or whatever you're calling yourself this week.

MILADY. Milady de Winter.

CARDINAL RICHELIEU. How chilling.

MILADY. Thank you. I'll intercept the letter, but my fee has doubled.

CARDINAL RICHELIEU. You're dreaming.

MILADY (*exiting*). You're so tiresome.

CARDINAL RICHELIEU. Okay fine! Double. But there's something else; Constance Bonacieux – the Queen's lady-in-waiting who has been entrusted with the delivery of this letter. I don't want her causing problems. She must be detained.

MILADY. You mean killed?

CARDINAL RICHELIEU. On no account must she die! I want her brought in for 'questioning'.

MILADY. You mean torture?

CARDINAL RICHELIEU. No, questioning! God, you're weird.

MILADY. That's rich, coming from a man who spends half his life in a cupboard perving over people's guilty secrets.

CARDINAL RICHELIEU. It's a confessional box!

MILADY. Have a nice afternoon, vicar.

CARDINAL RICHELIEU. Cardinal!

MILADY. Whatever.

She flicks her cigarette back into the room

CARDINAL RICHELIEU. Jesus! (*Crosses himself.*) Sorry, Father, please forgive me.

He turns and we see that MILADY *has stuck an 'I'm a Vicar' sign to his back.*

Scene Seven

SM *holds a dishevelled sign that reads 'Office of Captain Treville, the King's Musketeers'.*

D'ARTAGNAN. Hello? Captain Treville? Anyone here?

TREVILLE *is slumped at a table, clutching a half-empty bottle of spirits.*

Captain Treville?

TREVILLE. Ha! Captain? Used to be. The bastard has finally crippled us.

D'ARTAGNAN. What? Who?

TREVILLE. Cardinal Richelieu.

D'ARTAGNAN. Who's that?

TREVILLE. Who's Cardinal Richelieu? Do you have *any* awareness of French politics?

D'ARTAGNAN. Politics don't interest me. I've come to Paris to become a musketeer.

TREVILLE. You're too late. The musketeers are no more.

D'ARTAGNAN. But that can't be true. I've got a letter of introduction from my father, Charles Ogier de Batz.

TREVILLE. So, you're ol' Charlie's lad. Show me the letter.

D'ARTAGNAN. I can't. It was stolen from me last night by…

MILADY *has thrown a window to* D'ARTAGNAN *as she walks past.*

…that woman out on the street! Captain Treville, I will make it my life's mission to get that letter back and to reinstate the King's musketeers.

TREVILLE. You do that, kid! You do that.

D'ARTAGNAN *exits, after business with window.*

Scene Eight

ARAMIS *kneels to pray. In his chase,* D'ARTAGNAN *jumps into transept, disturbing him. They converse in hushed whisper.*

ARAMIS. What are you doing, you massive plonker! Forgive me, Father. (*Crosses himself.*)

D'ARTAGNAN. I defy any man to call me a massive plonker. Forgive me, Father. (*Crosses himself.*)

ARAMIS. You're a massive plonker. Forgive me again, Father. (*Crosses himself.*)

D'ARTAGNAN. Right! I'm going to track you down and kill you.

ARAMIS. I'm ready now.

D'ARTAGNAN. I'm afraid I'm in a bit of a hurry right now. But name a time and place and I'll be there.

ARAMIS. Okay, midday – behind Co-op.

D'ARTAGNAN. What's Co-op?

ARAMIS. The grocery market. By the bins.

D'ARTAGNAN. Co-op bin area it is!

D'ARTAGNAN departs.

ARAMIS. Forgive me, Father – couldn't be helped.

D'ARTAGNAN. Where did she go? There!

He chases MILADY *but disturbs* ATHOS, *who is having a drink at a bar, causing him to spill his drink.*

Sorry, mate.

ATHOS. Oi! I think you owe me another drink.

D'ARTAGNAN. It's still full.

ATHOS *throws the rest of his drink in* D'ARTAGNAN*'s face.*

ATHOS. It's not now.

D'ARTAGNAN. Oh, I don't think you meant to do that. Although I will offer you the opportunity to apologise.

ATHOS. And I'll offer you the opportunity to skip home for your tea before I run you through.

D'ARTAGNAN. It seems like you've just earned yourself a duel. One o'clock. Co-op bin area.

ATHOS. I'll look forward to it.

As he turns a corner, PORTHOS *is about to tuck into a big cream pie.*

D'ARTAGNAN. Out of my way please!

He leap-frogs over PORTHOS, *who is left with the pie in his face and down his front.*

Sorry. I'm in a real hurry.

PORTHOS. Do you have any idea how much this cape is worth?

D'ARTAGNAN. Not really.

PORTHOS. No, I don't suppose a yokel like you would.

D'ARTAGNAN. Is that some kind of veiled insult of my heritage?

PORTHOS. No, it's an open insult – of every ignoramus in your family, living and dead.

D'ARTAGNAN. No one but the King insults my family name. Two o'clock, Co-op bin area. Sorry, got to run.

He runs off and ends up alone on stage.

Merde! Where did she go?

Scene Nine

Co-op bin area. ATHOS, PORTHOS *and* ARAMIS *arrive.*
PORTHOS *and* ARAMIS *describe* D'ARTAGNAN's *appearance* (*dress, features of the actor, etc.*) *then...*

PORTHOS. Sounds like the same guy to me.

ARAMIS. Who the heck is he?

PORTHOS. I dunno, but I remember having that kind of lip once.

ARAMIS. So do I – you were a right bell-end!

PORTHOS. I'm afraid I'm going to have to kill you for that, Aramis.

ARAMIS. Might be tricky if you're already dead, Chunky.

They sword-fight.

ATHOS. Guys, please. I have a headache.

ARAMIS. What's up with him?

PORTHOS. A woman?

ARAMIS. There's no *woman* that can get under his skin. Not since... You-know-who.

PORTHOS. She *was* beautiful by all accounts.

ARAMIS. Piercing blue eyes, like alpine lakes, they say.

PORTHOS. And a massive brain.

ATHOS. I *can* hear you, you know! And I'll thank you never to mention her again.

ARAMIS. Athos, sending your wife to the gallows is a big deal, man. I think you've got some closure issues to work through.

ATHOS. Well I don't.

PORTHOS. In his defence though – I mean, if my missus had tried to kill me after I'd found out she'd garrotted her first husband for his inheritance.

ARAMIS. And *then* discovered she had the criminal branding of the fleur-de-lis.

PORTHOS. The most shameful mark a person in the sixteenth century /

ARAMIS. Seventeenth century.

PORTHOS. *Seventeenth century* can bear.

ATHOS. Have you quite finished with the expositional backstory of my wife?

PORTHOS. Yep.

ARAMIS. Yep.

PORTHOS. Ex-wife.

ARAMIS. Dead wife.

D'ARTAGNAN *arrives on his bike*.

PORTHOS. Aye, aye. Seems our date's arrived.

D'ARTAGNAN. What? Hang on, why are you *all* here?

PORTHOS. We're rarely separated.

D'ARTAGNAN. And… you're all musketeers!

ARAMIS. He's quick.

D'ARTAGNAN. As you're about to witness. Who's first?

ARAMIS. Me, me!

D'ARTAGNAN. I wouldn't be too eager if I were you.

PORTHOS. He'll be fine, he's got God on his side.

D'ARTAGNAN. Well let's hope God's good with a sword.

ATHOS. Step aside. I'll go first.

ATHOS *and* D'ARTAGNAN *fight*. ARAMIS *and*
PORTHOS *look on*.

ARAMIS. Blimey, this kid's good.

PORTHOS. Yeah. New belt, Athos?

ATHOS. Yep. Marks and Sparkles.

PORTHOS. Quality. I get all my underwear from there.

ARAMIS. Briefs or boxers?

PORTHOS. Briefs all the way, mate.

ARAMIS. Seriously? Don't you find they go up your /

PORTHOS. Arses! The Cardinal's men have spotted us.

ATHOS. Hey, kid, stop.

D'ARTAGNAN. Not until you surrender.

ATHOS. Oh shut up, you gobshite.

ARAMIS. Oh you're kidding – they're gonna try and arrest us
for duelling *again*?

ATHOS. There's about forty of them. And we're just three.

D'ARTAGNAN. No. Four.

ATHOS. This is not your affair, boy.

D'ARTAGNAN. I may not have the tunic, sir, but I have the
heart of a musketeer.

ATHOS. What's your name?

D'ARTAGNAN. D'Artagnan.

ATHOS. Well then, D'Artagnan. Let's see what you're really
made of.

The battle begins, during which they gradually become the CARDINAL'S GUARDS, *who we see losing, falling to the floor. Routine ends with just* CARDINAL'S GUARDS *lying wounded.*

GUARD 1. Where did they go?

GUARD 2. Ran off on their horses.

GUARD 3. Cowards. Didn't even kill us.

GUARD 4. Yeah. Idiots.

Blackout.

Scene Ten

The MUSKETEERS *arrive on their bikes in the den.*

PORTHOS. Well that seems to have perked someone up.

ATHOS. The sword is the only therapist I need. Now, hand over the money you stole, I mean took as compensation from the Cardinal's guards.

They place coins into a jar from their pockets. Except for D'ARTAGNAN.

D'ARTAGNAN. I don't steal.

PORTHOS. Yet.

ATHOS. Not a bad haul. D'Artagnan, welcome to the den. My name is Athos – oldest, wisest and basically leader of the musketeers.

ARAMIS. Former musketeers.

ATHOS. This is Aramis and our chunky friend here is Porthos.

D'ARTAGNAN. Wow! This place is awesome and you guys are as cool as.

ATHOS. And you're pretty handy with that sword.

PORTHOS. Just a shame your horse is so crap.

D'ARTAGNAN. Listen, will everyone stop slagging off my horse! My mum and dad gave him to me and it's all they had. And I really miss them!

ATHOS *motions to* PORTHOS.

PORTHOS. Hey. Sorry. Come on, put it there.

They fist-bump.

ATHOS. Thanks for helping us out back there. I'd say that makes us even.

D'ARTAGNAN. Okay great. I've got some special wound-healing cream my mum made if you want to put it on any sword cuts?

The others share a look, until…

ATHOS. Yeah why not. Thanks. Biscuit?

D'ARTAGNAN. Thanks.

ATHOS. Beer?

D'ARTAGNAN. Yeah! But I don't understand – why do the Cardinal's guards have it in for you?

ARAMIS. In a nutshell, because of our loyalty to the King.

D'ARTAGNAN. But isn't the Cardinal loyal to the King?

ATHOS. You have a lot to learn, my friend. The Cardinal seeks ultimate power over France. That's why he disbanded the musketeers.

D'ARTAGNAN. Well I've made it my mission to get them reinstated.

ATHOS. Ha! I like this guy.

He picks up the jar of money.

The musketeers' motto is 'all for one and one for all', which roughly translated means ten for me, ten for Aramis – to keep his mistresses happy, ten for Porthos – to keep him in cream horns, and ten for you to acquire some lodgings here in Paris.

D'ARTAGNAN. Thanks.

ATHOS. And the rest stays in the drinks jar.

THREE MUSKETEERS. Pub garden for beer and crisps. All for one and one for all!

D'ARTAGNAN....for all.

D'ARTAGNAN is left standing, jubilant, after the others exit. PORTHOS *returns.*

PORTHOS. You coming, mate?

D'ARTAGNAN. Yes.

Transition – sound effects of a bar. We hear/see much merriment. D'ARTAGNAN *stumbles out.*

PORTHOS (*off*). Hey! You're not leaving. Not yet.

D'ARTAGNAN. Seriously, guys – I have to find somewhere to sleep tonight.

ARAMIS. Try down Rue de Florentine. There's a ton of guesthouses.

Scene Eleven

D'ARTAGNAN *sees a 'vacancies' sign under '21 Rue de Florentine'.*

MONSIEUR BONACIEUX *sits behind the reception desk doing a crossword.*

MONSIEUR BONACIEUX. Eight down, 'Expression used to attract attention.'

D'ARTAGNAN (*approaching*). Excuse me?

MONSIEUR BONACIEUX. Correct, thanks. Now, nineteen across.

D'ARTAGNAN. I'm looking for a room.

M BONACIEUX. 'Likely phrase used by a person seeking lodgings.'

D'ARTAGNAN. No, listen, I actually want to rent a room.

MONSIEUR BONACIEUX. Oh I see. How does five francs a week sound?

D'ARTAGNAN. Great.

MONSIEUR BONACIEUX. Okay, how about six?

D'ARTAGNAN. Deal.

MADAME BONACIEUX (CONSTANCE) *rushes in from the street with a letter in her hand. She's very wary that she might have been followed.*

MONSIEUR BONACIEUX. Ah, you're back. This chap needs showing to his room.

CONSTANCE. Has the postman been yet?

MONSIEUR BONACIEUX. Yes, he came early. You alright?

CONSTANCE. Damn!

D'ARTAGNAN. Can I help?

CONSTANCE. Are you a postman?

D'ARTAGNAN. Alas, I'm not.

CONSTANCE. Then I'm afraid that you…

Dreamy moment when she turns to him.

Can't.

They're in their own bubble.

D'ARTAGNAN. But if I *were* in the service of *La Poste*, the opportunity to transport your letters would alone make the job worthwhile.

CONSTANCE. In that case, I might be tempted to use *La Poste* more frequently.

D'ARTAGNAN. Then I would spend my days hoping that one day, one of your letters might be addressed to me – 'To The Postman'.

CONSTANCE. Au facteur.

D'ARTAGNAN. Who waits.

CONSTANCE. Le facteur attend.

D'ARTAGNAN. For a letter.

CONSTANCE. Pour une lettre.

D'ARTAGNAN. From the most beautiful woman he'd ever set eyes upon.

CONSTANCE. De la plus belle femme qu'il ait jamais vue…

MONSIEUR BONACIEUX. But he's not a postman, is he – he's just some bloke who wants to rent a room off'f us!

CONSTANCE. Yes, of course you are. I mean, do. Is! Sorry. Look I'm not here, okay. If anyone comes asking for me – whoever they say they are – just explain that I'm not here.

MONSIEUR BONACIEUX. What's going on?

CONSTANCE. Nothing. Nothing. I'll be downstairs. But I won't be! Please, it's very important.

MONSIEUR BONACIEUX. But he has to be shown his room. And what with those stairs and my bowels.

CONSTANCE. Give me the key. Follow me, sir.

They head up the stairs.

D'ARTAGNAN. I take it that's your husband.

She looks back at her husband, who belches.

CONSTANCE. Oui. C'est une tragédie.

They continue upstairs. MILADY *enters below.*

MONSIEUR BONACIEUX. 'Cunning and devious, twelve letters.'

MILADY. Manipulative.

MONSIEUR BONACIEUX. Yes.

MILADY. Are you the husband of Constance Bonacieux, lady-in-waiting to Queen Anne?

MONSIEUR BONACIEUX. Might be. But she's not here. Who are you?

MILADY. I'm here to warn you that someone is about to try and kidnap her.

MONSIEUR BONACIEUX. What?

MILADY. So listen very carefully. This 'someone' is obviously not just going to walk in here, like I've just done, and ask to see your wife because you'll say…

MONSIEUR BONACIEUX. She's not here.

MILADY. So instead they'll try to *trick* you. But don't be fooled!

MONSIEUR BONACIEUX. I won't be.

MILADY. So I can trust you to protect her?

MONSIEUR BONACIEUX. Of course.

MILADY. And inform her of the danger?

MONSIEUR BONACIEUX. Absolutely.

MILADY. And not reveal her whereabouts to anyone suspicious.

MONSIEUR BONACIEUX. I'm not stupid.

MILADY. Good. So where is she?

MONSIEUR BONACIEUX. Upstairs.

MILADY. Excellent. Call her down now but keep it vague or she'll think something's amiss. Go!

He heads to the stairs.

MONSIEUR BONACIEUX. Constance?

MILADY. Tell her you need assistance.

MONSIEUR BONACIEUX. I've shat myself again.

CONSTANCE (*off*). Okay, one moment.

MILADY. Now, go and fetch me a glass of water, it's so hot today.

MONSIEUR BONACIEUX. Is it?

MILADY. This is no time to argue about the weather, someone's trying to kidnap your wife!

He exits. MILADY *speaks to an unseen person at the entrance.*

Standby. She's heading down.

Meanwhile upstairs…

CONSTANCE. I hope you'll be very comfortable here, sir.

D'ARTAGNAN. D'Artagnan. I'm sure I will be, Madame…?

CONSTANCE. Call me Constance. Listen, I'm sorry about that business earlier. I don't know what came over me.

D'ARTAGNAN. Me too. I didn't realise you were married.

Pause.

CONSTANCE. I'm not really sorry.

D'ARTAGNAN. No, me neither.

They're about to kiss.

CONSTANCE. I have to go.

D'ARTAGNAN. Your letter. It sounds urgent.

CONSTANCE. I'm afraid I can't talk about it.

She heads downstairs.

D'ARTAGNAN. She's the loveliest creature I've ever set eyes upon!

A CARDINAL GUARD *has entered and been given instructions from* MILADY. *When* CONSTANCE *reaches the bottom of the stairs she is grabbed by him.* MILADY *takes the letter from* CONSTANCE*'s hand.* CONSTANCE *is wrestled away, but* D'ARTAGNAN *hears her exit scream and heads down, only to be knocked out by* MILADY. *He comes to as* MONSIEUR BONACIEUX *enters with a glass of water.*

MONSIEUR BONACIEUX. Where did she go?

D'ARTAGNAN. Where were you?

MONSIEUR BONACIEUX. The lady said she wanted a glass of water.

D'ARTAGNAN. Who? What lady?!

MONSIEUR BONACIEUX. She said my wife's life was in danger.

D'ARTAGNAN. Constance? Describe her.

MONSIEUR BONACIEUX. Well when we were first married…

D'ARTAGNAN. The other woman!

MONSIEUR BONACIEUX. She had these piercing blue eyes. Like alpine lakes.

D'ARTAGNAN (*to himself*). What?

MONSIEUR BONACIEUX. Very hypnotic, she was.

D'ARTAGNAN. It couldn't be the same woman. Could it?

MONSIEUR BONACIEUX. I've no idea. (*Calling.*) Constance?

D'ARTAGNAN. Monsieur Bonacieux, I believe your wife has been kidnapped.

MONSIEUR BONACIEUX. Oh great, that's all I flipping need!

D'ARTAGNAN. I will track down that woman with the blue alpine-lake eyes and I will find your gorgeous wife and I will marry her.

M BONACIEUX. Eh?

D'ARTAGNAN. Sorry, didn't mean to say that out loud. I need my musketeers!

Scene Twelve

MILADY (*face veiled*) *kneels in a confession box.* CARDINAL RICHELIEU *enters and sits on the other side of the curtain, where a goblet of wine has been left for him.*

CARDINAL RICHELIEU. Okay, begin.

He drinks the wine.

MILADY. Forgive me, Father, for I have sinned. It's been a week since my last…

CARDINAL RICHELIEU. Yes, yes, forget all that. Just tell me about any impure thoughts you've been having. And don't hold back.

MILADY. Wow, you really *are* an old perv, aren't you.

He pulls back the curtain and realises that it's MILADY.

CARDINAL RICHELIEU. You are bloody incorrigible!

MILADY. I have Queen Anne's letter to Lord Buckingham that you requested.

CARDINAL RICHELIEU. Give it here. (*Reads.*) Blah, blah, blah… This is useless! What can I do with this? It's just superficial pleasantries.

MILADY. So rewrite it.

CARDINAL RICHELIEU. What?

MILADY. Sex it up.

CARDINAL RICHELIEU. I have an even better idea – rewritten in the Queen's hand, the content will lure Lord Buckingham, the British Prime Minister, into a secret liaison with her. At the Louvre. A fake reply will come back to Queen Anne, seemingly from him, pleading to meet him at the same location. And bingo – I'll have all the evidence I need to bring her down.

MILADY. Good luck with that.

CARDINAL RICHELIEU. Oh, I won't be writing the letters. You will. You will then conceal yourself within their *lover's corner* and capture whatever passes between them.

MILADY. That's disgusting, I'm not doing that.

CARDINAL RICHELIEU. Whatever *words or items*. I need evidence! And if you get it wrong, you will die.

MILADY. That's brave talk for a man who's just drunk poison.

CARDINAL RICHELIEU. You absolute…!

He starts gagging and rolling around on the floor.

MILADY. I'll do what you ask. But if you want the antidote, you'd better agree to my new payment terms. Here.

She drops him a contract, which he signs. She throws him the bottled antidote, which he drinks and recovers.

CARDINAL RICHELIEU. You're insane! That wasn't funny.

MILADY. It was a bit. The letters will be delivered by tomorrow, vicar.

CARDINAL RICHELIEU. Cardinal! I will prevail!

She exits.

Scene Thirteen

The letters in transit being delivered – to BUCKINGHAM *in England, who is shooting grouse, with a sign above him that reads 'The British PM Lord Buckingham' and another to* QUEEN ANNE *with a sign that reads 'Queen Anne of France'. They are each very taken with the letters.* BUCKINGHAM *starts packing immediately.* QUEEN ANNE *throws on a coat and scarf and exits.*

Scene Fourteen

Night. D'ARTAGNAN *can't sleep. He goes to his window.*

D'ARTAGNAN. She's vanished but I see her everywhere –
every woman in a headscarf that turns a corner, every shawl
in the distance. I know it's madness but…

A woman fitting that description rushes past, below him.

Constance? Constance!

He chases and catches her up.

QUEEN ANNE (*Spanish accent*). Get your hands off me!

D'ARTAGNAN. Oh my God, you're…

QUEEN ANNE. No I'm not.

D'ARTAGNAN. You are.

QUEEN ANNE. I'm not, don't look at me.

D'ARTAGNAN. You're the Queen!

QUEEN ANNE. Alright, I am. But keep your voice down! Who
are you?

D'ARTAGNAN. D'Artagnan, Your Majesty – royal musketeer.
Well not exactly, but I hope to be.

QUEEN ANNE. I thought the musketeers had been disbanded.

D'ARTAGNAN. I have tasked myself with the job of getting
them reinstated.

QUEEN ANNE. Impressive.

D'ARTAGNAN. Thank you.

QUEEN ANNE. And quite sexy.

D'ARTAGNAN. Sorry?

QUEEN ANNE. Then perhaps you can do me a favour?

D'ARTAGNAN. Anything.

QUEEN ANNE. Escort me to the Louvre.

D'ARTAGNAN. Meh.

QUEEN ANNE. What is it?

D'ARTAGNAN. I'm not that keen on art.

QUEEN ANNE. I'm not asking you to accompany me to an exhibition, you moron!

D'ARTAGNAN. Oh good. Phew.

QUEEN ANNE. Let's go.

They arrive at the Louvre.

Can you wait?

D'ARTAGNAN. I won't move from this spot.

She heads upstairs. Split-stage story scene. BUCKINGHAM *appears. He makes his way to an upper level and then reads from his letter.*

BUCKINGHAM. Meet me in the Denon Wing. Room seventy-five. Where the hell is that?

MILADY *appears and steps behind a painting of a woman eavesdropping through a curtain.* (*Allowing for actor to quick-change into* QUEEN ANNE.) *Meanwhile, a* SECURITY GUARD *approaches* D'ARTAGNAN.

LOUVRE GUARD. Oi. Can you read?

D'ARTAGNAN. Yes. Can you?

LOUVRE GUARD. That sign says 'keep off the grass'.

D'ARTAGNAN. Well done. And can you write as well?

LOUVRE GUARD. Step away from the grass, sunshine.

D'ARTAGNAN. Who the hell do you think you are?

LOUVRE GUARD. The night-duty guard for the Louvre.

D'ARTAGNAN. I'm not going anywhere, mate.

They struggle. QUEEN ANNE *appears at the painting.* BUCKINGHAM *joins her. They lovingly embrace and converse.* MILADY*'s hands still 'appear' to be holding the painting she's hiding behind, eavesdropping.*

BUCKINGHAM. If it takes invading France to be with you, then it will be worthwhile. I am prepared to kill thousands to be in your arms, Anne.

QUEEN ANNE. Please, Georgie, it's too much.

BUCKINGHAM. Then run away with me.

QUEEN ANNE. No. I can't. I have to go.

BUCKINGHAM. Then give me some token of your love to hold on to until we meet again.

She takes off her necklace and hands it to BUCKINGHAM *with a kiss, and then exits and returns to* D'ARTAGNAN (*who has got rid of* GUARD).

QUEEN ANNE. Can you escort me back to the Palace?

D'ARTAGNAN. Of course.

They walk.

QUEEN ANNE. You will be paid for your services.

D'ARTAGNAN. I don't expect payment.

QUEEN ANNE. I insist. What's your address?

D'ARTAGNAN. 21 Rue de Florentine.

QUEEN ANNE. 21 Rue de Florentine?

D'ARTAGNAN. Yes. The property of Monsieur Bonacieux.

QUEEN ANNE. Good heavens. You're a tenant of my lady-in-waiting – Madame Bonacieux.

D'ARTAGNAN. Constance.

QUEEN ANNE. What a coincidence. How is she? I understand she has a fever.

D'ARTAGNAN. A fever? No, she's gone missing.

QUEEN ANNE. Missing?

D'ARTAGNAN. She was kidnapped three days ago. I've been searching Paris for her ever since.

QUEEN ANNE. What!?

D'ARTAGNAN. She was very anxious to deliver a letter.

QUEEN ANNE. My letter to Lord Buckingham! But if it was stolen, it means that the one he received from me was… a forgery. And therefore his reply to me was a forgery too! We've been set up. My diamonds!

D'ARTAGNAN. You've been robbed?

QUEEN ANNE. Worse. Come on.

D'ARTAGNAN. But what about Constance?

QUEEN ANNE. Don't worry. We'll find her.

Scene Fifteen

Night. Trumpet fanfare. Lights snap onto KING LOUIS, *creeping.*

COURTIER VOICE. His Royal Highness, King Louis the Thirteenth has risen.

Trumpet fanfare.

KING LOUIS. Stop it! Stop that racket!

Trumpets die out pathetically.

Blimey, can't even use the bathroom around here without some blessed fanfare announcing it!

CARDINAL RICHELIEU *enters.*

Here we go, stand by your beds – the boss has arrived.

CARDINAL RICHELIEU. Ha, ha. I wouldn't dream of placing myself in such light, Your Majesty.

KING LOUIS. I know, it was a joke. What are you implying?

CARDINAL RICHELIEU. Nothing. Nothing at all.

KING LOUIS. Gotcha! Relax, man.

CARDINAL RICHELIEU. Ha! Hilarious. You're up late.

KING LOUIS. Can't sleep. Tell me, are you and I doing a good job of running France? Because my wife's been giving me a right earful of late.

CARDINAL RICHELIEU (*terse*). Really.

KING LOUIS. She says the general mood is getting a bit too nationalistic; turning our noses up at our European neighbours – that sort of thing.

CARDINAL RICHELIEU. Which perhaps isn't surprising coming from a total... Spaniard.

A wolf-whistle.

KING LOUIS. What was that?

CARDINAL RICHELIEU. Will you excuse me for just one moment, Your Majesty?

KING LOUIS. I'll be in the bog.

Trumpets sound.

Enough with the trumpets!

CARDINAL RICHELIEU *departs to meet* MILADY, *outside.*

CARDINAL RICHELIEU. Well? What did you discover?

MILADY. –

CARDINAL RICHELIEU. Listen, you're not getting any more money out of me.

MILADY. I don't want money. I want a puppy.

CARDINAL RICHELIEU. Fine, I'll get you a puppy.

MILADY. In a ring.

CARDINAL RICHELIEU. A puppy in a ring? Don't be absurd.

MILADY. –

CARDINAL RICHELIEU. Alright! I'll get you a flipping puppy in a ring. Well?

MILADY. Queen Anne has given Lord Buckingham her diamond necklace as a keepsake.

CARDINAL RICHELIEU. Oh my. Oh my, that is good. Standby. I'll be in touch.

He heads back upstairs. Sound effect: toilet flush. KING LOUIS *enters.*

CARDINAL RICHELIEU *smiles.*

KING LOUIS. What?

CARDINAL RICHELIEU. I'm sure it's nothing, Sire.

KING LOUIS. What's nothing?

CARDINAL RICHELIEU. I honestly don't know any more than you do.

KING LOUIS. About what!?

CARDINAL RICHELIEU. Your wife parting with her diamond necklace.

KING LOUIS. The one I gave her as a wedding gift?!

CARDINAL RICHELIEU. Well you clearly know far more about the affair than I do.

KING LOUIS. What affair?

CARDINAL RICHELIEU. The necklace is bound to be in her room.

KING LOUIS. Not if she gave it away.

CARDINAL RICHELIEU. To her lover, you mean?

KING LOUIS. What lover?

CARDINAL RICHELIEU. Well if you're asking for a list of potential candidates, I'd say Lord Buckingham definitely *wouldn't* be on it.

KING LOUIS. Lord Buckingham?

CARDINAL RICHELIEU. Although now you put it like that. My goodness, you'd never be able to trust her again.

KING LOUIS. This is unbelievable.

CARDINAL RICHELIEU. But I'm sure the necklace isn't missing. And therefore a strip-search of her quarters will be completely unnecessary.

KING LOUIS. Guards! Strip-search the Queen's quarters and leave no drawer unturned. If that necklace can't be found there'll need to be some big answers to some big questions!

A COURTIER *enters to help search* QUEEN ANNE*'s quarters – clothes fly everywhere.*

Anything?

COURTIER. Nothing.

KING LOUIS. Then I can draw only one conclusion...

QUEEN ANNE *enters, furious.*

QUEEN ANNE. And what conclusion is that!?

KING LOUIS. Anne!

QUEEN ANNE. What on earth is going on?

KING LOUIS. Where's the diamond necklace I gave you as a wedding gift!?

QUEEN ANNE. At the diamond-necklace cleaning and polishing shop!

KING LOUIS. Oh. Is it?

QUEEN ANNE. How dare you. Yes, I'm looking at you, courtier.

COURTIER. I was just following orders.

QUEEN ANNE. Clear up this mess and get out of my bedroom!

CARDINAL RICHELIEU. I did try to warn you against this course of action, Your Majesty.

QUEEN ANNE. Oh, I'm sure you did. You would have put the idea into his head, you pious little shrew.

KING LOUIS. I *can* come up with ideas of my own, you know!

QUEEN ANNE. Well in that case, work out how I'm going to regain any modicum of trust and respect for you!

KING LOUIS. Fine! I will. Cardinal, can I have a quick word? (*Leaving*.)

QUEEN ANNE. And where's my lady-in-waiting, Constance Bonacieux? Because I know she's not ill.

CARDINAL RICHELIEU. I imagine she'll be back at home now, Your Majesty.

QUEEN ANNE. Now you've finished using her, you mean?

CARDINAL RICHELIEU. I'm sure I *don't* know what you mean.

She exits.

KING LOUIS. Merde! How did that happen?

CARDINAL RICHELIEU. You had no choice under the circumstances.

KING LOUIS. Well the circumstances now, are that I have to find a way out of the doghouse.

CARDINAL RICHELIEU. How about a dance?

KING LOUIS. Not now, I need to think.

CARDINAL RICHELIEU. No. I mean, how about organising a grand ball. In her honour.

KING LOUIS. OMG.

CARDINAL RICHELIEU. It would be the perfect occasion for her to wear the 'freshly polished' necklace. And then the whole sordid business of her alleged liaison with Lord Buckingham can be put to bed. No pun intended.

KING LOUIS. None taken.

CARDINAL RICHELIEU. But the sooner the better, I'd say. Saturday night for example.

KING LOUIS. But that's in four days' time!

CARDINAL RICHELIEU. You're right. Better bring it forward. Friday it is. I'll make the announcement in the morning.

He writes a letter.

Milady de Winter. Your fee is tripled. You will take a boat to England where you will 'fall in' with Lord Buckingham. From the Queen's necklace, in his possession, you will 'obtain' two of the twelve diamond stones and return immediately to France. (*To audience*.) So, even if the Queen manages to have the necklace returned in time, her inability to account for the missing stones will destroy her regardless!

Scene Sixteen

QUEEN ANNE. A ball? In three days' time? With Buckingham and the necklace now back in England? I'm lost. I'm sunk. Unless… D'Artagnan!

A summer's day. D'ARTAGNAN *enters with a picnic basket. He lays out a spread.* DAN *enters with a sun which gets caught in a tree – he ends up ripping it apart.* CONSTANCE *enters and places her hands over* D'ARTAGNAN's *eyes. They embrace and dance.*

CONSTANCE. Talk to me in poetic verse, D'Artagnan.

D'ARTAGNAN. I'm sure I can't, Constance.

CONSTANCE. I don't believe that. You're wonderful in every other way.

D'ARTAGNAN. Umm…

CONSTANCE. And make it rhyme.

D'ARTAGNAN. I saw a cow,
    I don't know how,
    The milk comes from its udder.
    But like a boat,
    It stays afloat,
    Because it's got a rudder?

CONSTANCE. That's amazing. You just made that up?

D'ARTAGNAN. Yes. But I'm really no poet. I'm just a man who is tongue-tied by your beauty, who lives for your every glance, who yearns for your love, who wishes that your waste-of-space husband would die in some kind of shipping accident.

CONSTANCE. Oh, D'Artagnan, that's so romantic!

D'ARTAGNAN. Constance!

They kiss. A MESSENGER *enters.*

MESSENGER. A-hem.

D'ARTAGNAN. Yes?

MESSENGER. The Queen requests to see D'Artagnan immediately.

CONSTANCE. It could be a new assignment. Come on.

D'ARTAGNAN (*to* MESSENGER). Clear this up.

MESSENGER. I'm a messenger. It's not my job.

CONSTANCE. Clean it up or I'll have you fired, you little twerpington!

MESSENGER. [Fu]ck's sake.

CONSTANCE. Without the attitude! (*Cuffs him.*)

D'ARTAGNAN *arrives in court while the* MESSENGER *is obliged to strike the picnic.*

D'ARTAGNAN. Your Majesty.

QUEEN ANNE. Thank you for coming so quickly. And thank you for your previous concern over Constance. I'm sure you're aware of her return.

D'ARTAGNAN. I am, yes.

QUEEN ANNE. She's quite a woman.

D'ARTAGNAN. I've never met anyone like her. It's like I was blind to the way of the world before we met.

QUEEN ANNE. Right. And I expect her husband's relieved to see her too.

D'ARTAGNAN. That layabout doesn't deserve her.

QUEEN ANNE. No. Perhaps not. Well, I'm certainly glad we can converse so frankly with one another, D'Artagnan, because I have a very personal matter I need to discuss with you. I'm in trouble, you see. Really big trouble.

D'ARTAGNAN. Okay. So how late are you?

QUEEN ANNE. What?

D'ARTAGNAN. You know – with your...

QUEEN ANNE. You forget yourself, sir!

D'ARTAGNAN. Please accept my apology. I've clearly misread the situation.

QUEEN ANNE. Indeed you have. Now listen, I need you to travel to England...

Transition to:

Scene Seventeen

The musketeers' den. D'ARTAGNAN *rushes to the cup phone.*

D'ARTAGNAN. Musketeers, this is a red alert. Do you copy? We have a mission.

ATHOS *and* ARAMIS *arrive on their bikes.*

ATHOS. What's going on, D'Artagnan?

D'ARTAGNAN. Where's Porthos?

ARAMIS. On his way.

He arrives hurriedly from his quick-change. He still has a wig on, which he whips off.

D'ARTAGNAN. Gentlemen, we have an assignment issued direct from Her Majesty the Queen.

PORTHOS. The actual Queen!? Seriously?

ARAMIS. He's winding us up.

D'ARTAGNAN. I'm not.

ATHOS. What is it, D'Artagnan?

D'ARTAGNAN. We must travel to England to retrieve a necklace she wants to wear to a ball.

Pause.

PORTHOS. That sooo is a wind-up.

ARAMIS. Seriously, mate – that's so lame.

D'ARTAGNAN. I'm being serious!

ATHOS. I believe him! This can't simply be about a woman's whim for a certain fashion accessory. The very stability of the royal court must be at stake. Am I right, D'Artagnan?

D'ARTAGNAN. You are.

ATHOS. Yesss! Get in.

ARAMIS. That doesn't change the fact though that we – the most skilled and feared swordsmen in France – have been assigned to fetch a flipping necklace.

PORTHOS. Would she like us to pick up her dry cleaning too?

ATHOS. Will you two put your egos to one side for a moment. This could be the start of the King's musketeers being reinstated. This is our moment. This is our perfect moment, with you. Sorry, a little song idea just popped into my head.

PORTHOS *has wandered off.*

What is it, Porthos?

PORTHOS. No, it's fine.

ATHOS. There are no secrets among the musketeers.

PORTHOS. It's just that – I mean, nothing against D'Artagnan but, you know, this kid arrives in Paris, he's not even a musketeer and suddenly it's like 'D'Artagnan the saviour'.

ATHOS. Your point being?

PORTHOS. Just takes a bit of getting used to, that's all.

ATHOS. Well get used to it pronto.

D'ARTAGNAN. It's a shock to me too, Porthos. But the bottom line is this – I just think you guys are awesome!

PORTHOS. Okay, sweet. Let's smash this!

ALL. All for one and one for all!

Scene Eighteen

AL *addresses the audience*.

AL. Okay, everyone following? All clear so far? Good. So this is the bit where we need your help. Madame, can you please give me your impression of a duck? But not just a generic duck. Specifically, a mallard. (*She does*.) Okay, that's terrible.

EMMA. Don't worry we have these – (*Hands out duck whistles to front row*.) Now, when we give you the signal you have to blow. Okay? Quick trial? Great.

AL. And when you hear the ducks, you lot have to throw these on stage.

He hurls loads of ducks into the audience.

Got it? Good. We transport you to England and the estate of the British PM, Lord Buckingham.

BUCKINGHAM *is shooting.* MILADY *approaches, lights a cigarette and watches.*

BUCKINGHAM. Good afternoon.

MILADY (*Russian accent*). Looks fun.

BUCKINGHAM. Best sport in the world. Ever tried?

MILADY. Killing?

BUCKINGHAM. Hell of a rush.

MILADY. I can imagine.

BUCKINGHAM *offers her the gun.*

BUCKINGHAM. It's quite straightforward. You take a firm grip of the shaft and when you hear a ducky wucky, you simply cock, aim and fire.

She takes the gun.

AL. Ducks, now!

Audience make duck noises. MILADY *expertly shoots ducks that are thrown onto the stage.*

BUCKINGHAM. Well bugger me!

MILADY. You're right, that's some rush. Wooeee! I don't quite know what to do with myself now.

BUCKINGHAM. Where are you from?

MILADY. Russia. I'm staying with an aunt in London but she's so boring. I needed some fun. So I jumped on the first train and ended up here. Have I come to the right place?

BUCKINGHAM. You most certainly have. This is my estate.

MILADY. All this land?

BUCKINGHAM. Far as the eye can see. And all the buildings.

MILADY. Including that one.

BUCKINGHAM. The woodshed?

MILADY. What's a woodshed?

BUCKINGHAM. I'll show you.

Blackout. Rush of jungle sounds, sirens, train going through tunnel, hallelujah chorus. MILADY *emerges looking relaxed.* BUCKINGHAM *emerges looking dishevelled with twigs in his hair, exhausted.*

MILADY. I'd better get back to London.

BUCKINGHAM. Will I see you again?

MILADY. I'm not sure that's such a good idea. That necklace you're wearing looks like a gift from someone special.

BUCKINGHAM. Yes. Very special, in fact.

MILADY. I wouldn't like to come between you.

TORQUIL (*off*). Georgie? Georgie, where are you, old chap?

TORQUIL *enters*.

BUCKINGHAM. Torquil. What is it?

TORQUIL. Thank goodness! We wondered where you'd got to.

BUCKINGHAM. I was just… checking on the wood supply.

TORQUIL. We're all headed to The Dog and Trumpet to get spiffed. Coming?

BUCKINGHAM. Too right. And perhaps… where did she go?

TORQUIL. You alright, chap?

BUCKINGHAM. Yes. Yes, I'm fine.

TORQUIL. Well come on then.

They exit. MILADY *steps out from the shadows and inspects two diamonds.*

MILADY. Very pretty indeed.

Scene Nineteen

Sounds of rowdy bar with drinking songs. BUCKINGHAM *is stood on a table leading the rabble (basically* TORQUIL).

Song.

Oh, one day in May when Mary lay a-sleeping
Along came a corporal on hands and knees a-creeping
With his long funny dingle-dangle
Way down to his knees.

D'ARTAGNAN *rushes in.*

D'ARTAGNAN. Excuse me. Excuse me!? I was told Lord
  Buckingham might be here.

TORQUIL. And who might you be?

D'ARTAGNAN. D'Artagnan. From France.

TORQUIL. Oooh. Parlez-vous Anglais?

D'ARTAGNAN. Er... Yes, I'm speaking it now.

TORQUIL. Hey – what's the difference between French men
  and toast? You can make soldiers out of toast.

D'ARTAGNAN. I must speak to Lord Buckingham. It's urgent.

BUCKINGHAM. I'm Lord Buckingham. State your affairs.

D'ARTAGNAN. One mistress, but we've only kissed.

BUCKINGHAM. Your business affairs, man! Go and get
  another round in, will you, Torquil. Well?

D'ARTAGNAN. I'm on an errand from Queen Anne of France.

BUCKINGHAM. How dare you presume to know Queen Anne
  of France.

D'ARTAGNAN. Why?

BUCKINGHAM. Because – (*Can't think.*) How do I know
  you're on an errand from her?

D'ARTAGNAN. I've just told you.

BUCKINGHAM. Apart from that!

D'ARTAGNAN. I know about your diamond necklace.

BUCKINGHAM. How could you possibly know about that?

D'ARTAGNAN. Because I'm on an errand from Queen Anne.

BUCKINGHAM. What errand?

D'ARTAGNAN. To get it back.

BUCKINGHAM. You're lying!

D'ARTAGNAN. Prove it.

BUCKINGHAM. What?

D'ARTAGNAN. Prove I'm lying.

BUCKINGHAM. Prove you're *not* lying first and then I'll prove you are, sir.

D'ARTAGNAN….Right. I know Queen Anne gave you the necklace in the Louvre as a gift.

BUCKINGHAM. Why would she divulge such intimate information to you?

D'ARTAGNAN. Because she thought you'd act like this.

BUCKINGHAM. Like what?

D'ARTAGNAN. Shouty and suspicious.

BUCKINGHAM. Why does she want the necklace back?

D'ARTAGNAN. For a ball the King is throwing for her in two days' time to apologise for suspecting she's having an affair.

BUCKINGHAM. Who with?

D'ARTAGNAN. You. Even though she is.

BUCKINGHAM. Who told you that?

D'ARTAGNAN. Constance.

BUCKINGHAM. Who the hell is Constance when she's at home?

D'ARTAGNAN. My mistress. And at work she's the Queen's lady-in-waiting. The Queen gave her a letter to post to you, but it was snatched.

BUCKINGHAM. The letter inviting me to the Louvre?

D'ARTAGNAN. No, the letter inviting you to the Louvre replaced the snatched letter, but little did you know it was a forgery from the Cardinal who made it appear as if was from the Queen.

BUCKINGHAM. What?

D'ARTAGNAN. And the Queen was sent a corresponding letter from you, asking to meet her at the Louvre too.

BUCKINGHAM. I never sent a letter?

D'ARTAGNAN. No, because the Cardinal forged that one as well! Well more likely his aide did.

BUCKINGHAM. What aide?

D'ARTAGNAN. A beautiful but incredibly dangerous woman with eyes the colour of alpine lakes, who I believe is on her way here now to try and steal the necklace.

BUCKINGHAM. Oh sh… she's not Russian, is she?

D'ARTAGNAN. She could be Russian if she wanted.

BUCKINGHAM. How do I know you're not lying?

D'ARTAGNAN. Will you please get over the lying thing! The Cardinal wishes to expose your affair. The Queen is distraught. Has that woman been here!?

BUCKINGHAM. The necklace is safe.

D'ARTAGNAN. Is it!?

BUCKINGHAM. You think I can't keep a necklace safe? Look.

D'ARTAGNAN. Thank goodness. Hang on…

BUCKINGHAM. Oh. My. Days! There are two diamonds missing! But it's been round my neck the whole time!

D'ARTAGNAN. Apart from when she had her way with you.

BUCKINGHAM. How dare you! (*Breaking down.*) How could I have been so foolish?

D'ARTAGNAN. You had no choice. She's as cunning as a fox, as slippery as an eel and as dangerous as a golden poison dart frog. We need the greatest jeweller in the country here, immediately.

BUCKINGHAM. Find him!

JEWELLER *enters.*

JEWELLER. Her, actually. Sexist.

BUCKINGHAM. Madame, I require you to cut two diamonds to match the stones in this necklace. How long will it take?

JEWELLER. Two weeks.

BUCKINGHAM. Try two hours! Block the ports and search every passenger. D'Artagnan, I will charter you the fastest vessel available, to ship you from Dover to Calais. Unless you'd rather go Plymouth–Roscoff?

D'ARTAGNAN. No, Dover's cool.

BUCKINGHAM. The finished necklace must be around the Queen's neck by Friday at… what time's the ball, mate?

D'ARTAGNAN. Seven for seven-thirty.

BUCKINGHAM. Seven for seven-thirty! People, let's kick this thing in the dick and make it happen!

The sails are hoisted, the JEWELLER *works frantically. The stones are handed to* D'ARTAGNAN *as he boards the ship. We set sail back to France,* D'ARTAGNAN *looks out to sea and sings.* CONSTANCE *appears in a dream and duets with him.*

D'ARTAGNAN.
Guided by the Northern Star
I see French shores in view
To England I've bid au revoir
I'm sailing home to you.

I love thee to the breadth and height
that my soul can reach you're delight-ful.

BOTH.
Before we met I was at sea
Now you're my land and keystone
Your smile means more than life to me
Your touch tells me that I am home.

So blow, fair wind, my love's in sight
I'll lie in your arms tonight.

Your kiss means more than life to me
Your touch tells me that I am home.

Over the end of the song, MILADY *enters and hands the* CARDINAL RICHELIEU *two diamonds.*

CARDINAL RICHELIEU. Yes!

He laughs hysterically. Music reaches a crescendo.

Blackout.

Interval.

ACT TWO

Option for informal business with cast, chatting to the audience to make sure they're following the plot, setting costumes for Act Two.

Scene Twenty

The grand ball.

Spotlight on QUEEN ANNE, *frantically pacing.*

Spotlight on KING LOUIS, *exasperated, waiting for* QUEEN ANNE.

Spotlight on D'ARTAGNAN, *frantically cycling on a bike stand to a seventies' funk soundtrack.*

KING LOUIS. Darling, where are you? The guests have started to arrive.

QUEEN ANNE. D'Artagnan, where are you!? Be down in a moment, darling.

CARDINAL RICHELIEU *enters and stands, smugly.*

KING LOUIS. What?

CARDINAL RICHELIEU. I'm sure there's a simple explanation.

KING LOUIS. To what!?

CARDINAL RICHELIEU *opens a box he's holding.*

CARDINAL RICHELIEU. To why these two stones would be missing from the Queen's twelve-stoned diamond necklace. But I'm sure all will come to light when she emerges.

KING LOUIS. Anne?

QUEEN ANNE. I've told you, I'm coming!

KING LOUIS. Right, that does it.

He starts to head up towards her. At this moment,
D'ARTAGNAN *springs up to* QUEEN ANNE*'s level and*
climbs through her window.

Musical flourish.

QUEEN ANNE. D'Artagnan.

He hands her a box.

Milk Tray? Where's the flipping necklace?

D'ARTAGNAN. Sorry. Here.

He hands her another box containing the necklace.

There were two stones missing.

QUEEN ANNE. What!?

D'ARTAGNAN. That we replaced.

QUEEN ANNE. I owe you my life.

KING LOUIS. Anne?

QUEEN ANNE. Hide!

KING LOUIS *enters just as she gets the necklace on and*
D'ARTAGNAN *has climbed out of the window.*

Ta-daar!

KING LOUIS. You're wearing my wedding gift.

QUEEN ANNE. As you requested.

KING LOUIS. Permit me if you will to observe it more closely.

He quickly counts to twelve in French.

Cardinal?

CARDINAL RICHELIEU. Your Majesty?

KING LOUIS. Would you mind joining us?

CARDINAL RICHELIEU, *who's been listening, enters.*

Doesn't my wife look beautiful?

CARDINAL RICHELIEU. She does.

KING LOUIS. Ravishing you might you say?

CARDINAL RICHELIEU. That's not for me to say.

QUEEN ANNE. Make him say it.

KING LOUIS. Say it.

CARDINAL RICHELIEU. You look ravishing, Your Majesty.

QUEEN ANNE. How ravishing?

CARDINAL RICHELIEU. Very.

QUEEN ANNE. Only very?

CARDINAL RICHELIEU. Extremely.

QUEEN ANNE. I think you mean unbearably.

CARDINAL RICHELIEU. You look unbearably ravishing, Your Majesty.

QUEEN ANNE. Which can't be an easy sight for a man touching cloth, I mean *of the cloth*, like you.

KING LOUIS. Cardinal, would you care to count the stones in my wife's necklace.

CARDINAL RICHELIEU. Gladly.

He quickly counts to twelve in French, then says in shock…

There appear to be twelve.

KING LOUIS. A full house then. The full packet. So what are the two diamonds you've just shown me?

CARDINAL RICHELIEU. These are… a gift. I felt rather too embarrassed to offer them directly and without your consent so…

QUEEN ANNE. Oh you poor, coy old thing. That's so sweet. And I have a gift back to you. Just arrived by courier from England.

CARDINAL RICHELIEU. Milk Tray. I'm flattered.

KING LOUIS. Right! All sorted. To the ball!

KING LOUIS *and* QUEEN ANNE *exit*.

Scene Twenty-One

CARDINAL RICHELIEU. Milk Tray? She knows I'm lactose intolerant! What thorn was behind this? What thistle, what barb, what prick? Who was it!?

CARDINAL RICHELIEU *hurls the chocolates into the wings.* MILADY *appears.*

You failed.

MILADY. You mean, someone replaced the missing stones. Who was it? (*Beat.*) You don't know, do you.

CARDINAL RICHELIEU. I'll be in touch if I need you.

MILADY. You're dropping me? I have financial obligations to meet.

CARDINAL RICHELIEU. What on earth do you spend all my money on?

MILADY. Eggcups.

CARDINAL RICHELIEU. Like I say, I'll be in touch if I need you, Milady.

MILADY. Oh you'll need me. And when you do, my fee will be eye-watering.

She exits.

CARDINAL RICHELIEU. Enough of this *tame meddling.* The Queen's influence over the King and her agitation for *European unity* must be crushed once and for all. What can I do? I have it! Simply provoke an uprising I can then defeat and the people of France will love me. Or even better – a holy war. If I fire up the Protestant minority in La Rochelle, Lord Buckingham will come running to their aid from England. But he will meet his maker on French soil. Two birds. One stone. (*To audience.*) Don't worry if you can't keep up. You'll see soon enough. I will prevail!

Transition – suggestion of uprising, war, conflict.

Scene Twenty-Two

KING LOUIS *enters*.

KING LOUIS. Cardinal, I want my musketeers back on the payroll.

CARDINAL RICHELIEU. Why would you want that, Your Majesty? They've disbanded themselves.

KING LOUIS. You mean, *you* disbanded them.

CARDINAL RICHELIEU. For constantly fighting in the streets. They're rogue vigilantes. A law unto themselves.

KING LOUIS. Who will at least help defeat this curiously sudden uprising in La Rochelle.

CARDINAL RICHELIEU. I have that in order, Your Majesty. Don't you worry about that.

KING LOUIS. Really?

CARDINAL RICHELIEU. Oh yes.

KING LOUIS. Impressive.

CARDINAL RICHELIEU. It will be.

KING LOUIS. Nevertheless, there's another reason: my wife says she feels unsafe here in Paris. To the extent that she's been keeping a few former musketeers in service from the royal purse, I've discovered!

CARDINAL RICHELIEU (*aside*). So that explains the return of the necklace! (*To* KING LOUIS.) Queen Anne is becoming quite… strident, Your Majesty.

KING LOUIS. Tell me about it.

CARDINAL RICHELIEU. Well naturally, if some of these 'rogue musketeers' have been assisting her, then I should be thanking them personally. What are their names?

QUEEN ANNE *passes below*.

KING LOUIS. Hey, darling, what's the name of that musketeer chap that Constance fancies?

QUEEN ANNE. I'm sure I don't know what you're referring to, my love.

KING LOUIS. Yes you do. I overheard you both giggling like chimps the other day. He's lodging in her house. Got three friends he knocks about with. Call themselves the four musketeers.

QUEEN ANNE. I have no recollection of that conversation.

KING LOUIS. What?

QUEEN ANNE. Darling, I've given you my answer and if you carry on insisting you're going to make me late for my 'How to Win Negotiations with Your Husband' class. Is that what you want?

KING LOUIS. No.

QUEEN ANNE. Good.

She exits.

KING LOUIS. She does love that class. Can't see it does her a scrap of good though. So, I'll leave all this with you?

CARDINAL RICHELIEU. I will talk to Captain Treville and see if he can't do a better job of keeping a small, contained, band of musketeers in order.

KING LOUIS. Top notch. Back to my chess game. Thank you, Cardinal.

KING LOUIS *exits.*

CARDINAL RICHELIEU. And thank *you* – for exposing the Queen's diamond restorers. But they won't upset my plans a second time. If one of them is 'sweet' on Constance Bonacieux, if she were to take another little 'holiday', her disappearance will keep them fully occupied whilst I fan the flames of my uprising in La Rochelle. Because I can't risk them throwing water on that, can I, madame? Not before Buckingham is dead and the Queen's influence over the King is in tatters! I will prevail! Even more!

Scene Twenty-Three

The musketeers' den. PORTHOS *enters and talks into the cup phone.*

PORTHOS. Calling all musketeers, calling all musketeers!

ATHOS *arrives.*

ATHOS. Porthos, what is it?

PORTHOS. Ah nothing. I was just mucking about.

ATHOS. Well don't. This line is reserved for emergencies.

PORTHOS. What's up with you?

ATHOS. Nothing.

PORTHOS. Listen, I was thinking – it's just a thought but what if your ex-wife is still alive?

ATHOS. Impossible! She went to the gallows!

PORTHOS. But D'Artagnan's description of the woman with the piercing blue eyes like alpine lakes /

ATHOS. Is not the same person. End of!

ARAMIS *enters.* PORTHOS *distributes drinks.*

ARAMIS. What's happening? Who was on the cup phone?

ATHOS. Porthos. He was twotting about again.

ARAMIS. I was in the middle of praying.

PORTHOS. For what?

ARAMIS. Nothing specific. Just keeping my hand in, in case I ever return to the Church.

PORTHOS. You're a King's musketeer!

ARAMIS. Who no longer exist!

ATHOS. Perhaps not on a payroll, Aramis. But we exist in spirit. And we will rise again. That necklace mission was just the first step.

ARAMIS. And what a blast that turned out to be – I didn't even get to see England!

PORTHOS. Well if you will pick fights with everyone you meet.

ARAMIS. That innkeeper accused me of seducing his wife.

ATHOS. He caught you in bed with her.

ARAMIS. One time! Anyway, Porthos is the hot-headed one.

ATHOS. Only when he's hungry.

ARAMIS. He barricaded himself into a restaurant kitchen for three days in Lille!

PORTHOS. Has anyone seen my cream horn?

ATHOS. You're sat on it.

PORTHOS. Oh not again!

Pause.

ARAMIS. Has it dawned on anyone else that us 'Three Musketeers' are doing very little to actually drive the plot?

The other look very nervous.

ATHOS. Listen to me, you two – this is dangerous talk. It's the collective effort that counts. We just need another mission!

D'ARTAGNAN *enters.*

D'ARTAGNAN. Constance has been kidnapped!

PORTHOS, ARAMIS *and* ATHOS. Yes!

PORTHOS. Again? What is it with this woman?

D'ARTAGNAN. And Captain Treville has instructed us to find her.

He throws down a bag of coins.

ARAMIS. Captain Treville?

D'ARTAGNAN. He's ditched the booze and is working a recovery programme.

ATHOS (*raises cup*). To Captain Treville! Leader of the King's musketeers!

PORTHOS. Does this mean we're back in business?

ATHOS. Guys! I think Constance is the main focus here! But does it, D'Artagnan?

D'ARTAGNAN. It's beginning to look that way.

ATHOS. And if we can find Constance…?

D'ARTAGNAN. Exactly.

ATHOS. Yes! So, let's focus on what we already know. (*Beat.*) What do we already know?

D'ARTAGNAN. I'm convinced the Cardinal is behind this.

PORTHOS. Why? What's he trying to achieve?

ATHOS. Good question, Porthos.

ARAMIS. Maybe this is simply a plan to distract us while he gets on with something more sinister.

ATHOS. Excellent answer, Aramis. Grammatically pleasing too.

D'ARTAGNAN. So finding Constance quickly is of paramount importance.

ATHOS. Man, this discussion's got off to a good start!

They all look at ATHOS.

Sorry, I'm just feeling a bit… okay, very funny, who put coke in my grape juice again?

PORTHOS. A badger? Any idea where she's being held?

D'ARTAGNAN. No.

ATHOS. God, I'm buzzing.

D'ARTAGNAN. But I'm convinced the woman with alpine-lake eyes knows.

ARAMIS. Why?

D'ARTAGNAN. Cos she's clearly an extremely close ally of the Cardinal.

PORTHOS. Well she's hardly going to just *volunteer up* the information then, is she.

D'ARTAGNAN. And that's why I've formulated a plan, brilliant in its simplicity.

ATHOS. It's stunning! I love it. (*Beat*.) What is it?

D'ARTAGNAN. She falls in love.

PORTHOS. Who with?

D'ARTAGNAN *sticks on a moustache*.

D'ARTAGNAN. Me!

PORTHOS. But I thought you were in love with Constance?

D'ARTAGNAN. I am. Just let me finish /

ATHOS. But all they've done so far is kiss.

D'ARTAGNAN. Hey, that was confidential!

ATHOS. There are no secrets among the musketeers. He's also still a virgin.

D'ARTAGNAN. What the fu…!

ATHOS. Take a chill pill, D'Artagnan! Wow, I'm really flying now.

PORTHOS. So, if you've only kissed Constance, popping your cherry with Alpine-Lake Eyes won't even count as cheating.

ARAMIS. Is that how it works, Athos?

ATHOS. It's a grey area.

D'ARTAGNAN. Will you all shut up! I'm not going to sleep with her!

ARAMIS. Who, Constance?

D'ARTAGNAN. No!

PORTHOS. Hang on, I'm confused now.

ATHOS. For goodness' sake, people, wake up! The whole crux of D'Artagnan's plan is NOT to sleep with Alpine-Lake Eyes. But instead, to wind her up into such a fizz bomb of desire that she'll be ready to explode with all the information we need. Am I right? Yes I am. It's a plan worthy of the Bard himself.

ARAMIS. Is it?

ATHOS. Oh Christ, the comedown from this is gonna be massive.

ARAMIS. You're sure you're not just letting revenge cloud your vision here, D'Artagnan?

D'ARTAGNAN. No! This is absolutely the best way to rescue Constance.

PORTHOS. It's worth a shot I reckon. Where does she live?

D'ARTAGNAN. A château, somewhere in the Loire Valley.

ARAMIS. She really does sound a bit like your ex-wife, Athos.

ATHOS. For the last time, I hung my ex-wife! Let's go!

Routine to 'Crazy Horses' as they ride through the Loire Valley. ATHOS *gets a puncture.*

Guys, guys! My horse is lame. I'll catch up with you.

PORTHOS. See you in the next village.

The others ride on.

Scene Twenty-Four

They arrive in a clearing.

PORTHOS. This had better be it, cos if I see another flipping château.

D'ARTAGNAN. I'll meet you back at that inn we just passed if it is.

ARAMIS. May God be with you.

PORTHOS. Probably not the most helpful thought when he's about to drop his V-plates.

D'ARTAGNAN. For the last time, this is purely about finding Constance.

ARAMIS. And definitely not revenge, driven by infatuation?

D'ARTAGNAN. No!

D'ARTAGNAN *heads off*.

PORTHOS. It is though, isn't it.

ARAMIS. Yep.

D'ARTAGNAN *arrives at the door.*

KITTY. Oh hello.

She's immediately smitten.

D'ARTAGNAN. Hello. You work here, I presume?

KITTY. No I'm robbing the place. Jokes. I'm Kitty the maid.

D'ARTAGNAN. Hello, Kitty the maid. I'm looking for the lady of the house.

KITTY. Milady de Winter?

D'ARTAGNAN. All I know is that she has piercing blue eyes /

KITTY. Sounds like her.

D'ARTAGNAN. And an intoxicating presence /

KITTY. Definitely her.

D'ARTAGNAN. Like a wine you can't stop drinking, like…

KITTY. Yes, I think you've come to the right place! But she's not here at the moment. You can wait in the kitchen with me if you like – I'm just flouring my baps.

D'ARTAGNAN. I used to watch my mum do that. Any idea how long she'll be?

KITTY. Three days.

Sound effect: door slam followed by beginning of 'Rhapsody in Blue'. KITTY appears in a spot and writes…

'My dear sister, the most wondrous man has just walked into my life. I feel like we're destined to be together forever and I'm sure he feels the same way.'

Cut to D'ARTAGNAN *in the inn*.

D'ARTAGNAN. Oh shi…

PORTHOS. You haven't even met her yet?

D'ARTAGNAN. She's due back any minute now.

PORTHOS. So what have you been doing for the past three days!?

D'ARTAGNAN. The maid's *really* chatty.

PORTHOS. I'll bet she is.

D'ARTAGNAN. Porthos, it may be 1625, but it is possible to spend more than five minutes with a woman without trying to cop off.

PORTHOS. So your strategy with Milady de Winter hasn't been compromised at all?

D'ARTAGNAN. Okay, so Kitty may have become *a bit* sweet on me.

PORTHOS. How sweet?

D'ARTAGNAN. It's fine, I left her a note. She'll completely understand.

KITTY. You bastard!

D'ARTAGNAN *runs to* KITTY *and passes a man with long ginger locks and a handlebar moustache*.

COMTE DE WARDES. Evening.

D'ARTAGNAN. Evening.

COMTE DE WARDES. Lovely night for it.

COMTE DE WARDES *exits*.

D'ARTAGNAN. Weirdo.

He arrives to KITTY.

Kitty, let me explain.

KITTY. You're just like all the rest – using me to get to Milady de Winter!

D'ARTAGNAN. I promise you, my interest in her is purely administrative. By the way is she back yet?

KITTY. Well don't worry about me. Because I've thought of a simple way to overcome this rejection.

D'ARTAGNAN. That's the spirit.

KITTY. I'm going to kill myself.

D'ARTAGNAN. No!

KITTY. And good luck. Because Milady has a new lover.

D'ARTAGNAN. The guy who just left? What's his name?

KITTY. The Comte de Wardes. Why?

D'ARTAGNAN. Back in a tick.

KITTY. I'm destined to be a spinster forever.

Back at the inn.

ARAMIS. She has a lover? Well that's put a spanner in your plan.

D'ARTAGNAN. Exactly. So I've thought of a new one.

ARAMIS. Good.

D'ARTAGNAN. You disguise yourself as him.

ARAMIS. What?

D'ARTAGNAN. You happen to look uncannily like him already and who else is Milady going to divulge Constance's whereabouts to if not to her lover?

ARAMIS. Are you mental!?

D'ARTAGNAN. Oh and I suppose you could come up with a better idea?

ARAMIS. I think I could come up with a better idea if the ideas man in my head had shot himself because his office was flooded with blancmange.

D'ARTAGNAN *forces* ARAMIS *into the* COMTE DE WARDES's *jacket* (*or similar*).

D'ARTAGNAN. Aramis, the future of the musketeers is at stake! Not to mention Constance's safety!

ARAMIS. I'll never get away with it.

D'ARTAGNAN. Ah, but here's the clever bit – you will.

He pushes ARAMIS *towards the château and rings the doorbell.*

MILADY. Kitty?

KITTY. Got it, Milady.

D'ARTAGNAN *dresses* ARAMIS *in wig and moustache as* KITTY *heads for the door.*

ARAMIS. I must be mad. I *am* mad.

D'ARTAGNAN. By the way, he's got a very deep voice.

ARAMIS. Oh great!

D'ARTAGNAN. And might be Dutch.

ARAMIS (*leaving*). Right, that's it!

KITTY. Comte de Wardes?

ARAMIS. Yep. That's me.

KITTY. Did you forget something?

ARAMIS. No. I just couldn't stand being away from her.

KITTY. So romantic.

MILADY *appears at the top of the stairs.*

MILADY. I thought you were tied up for the week.

ARAMIS. Yeah well those stupid engagements mean nothing to me.

MILADY. Your mother's funeral?

ARAMIS. Yep.

MILADY. That's really sexy.

ARAMIS. Can I just ask you a question?

MILADY. No. Come here!

Blackout. Train in tunnel, jungle screeching, etc. Lights up on MILADY *smoking.* ARAMIS *is exhausted.*

Blimey. Where did *that* come from?

ARAMIS. I'm not sure.

D'ARTAGNAN (*below window*). Stick to the plan, Aramis. Just ask her where Constance is.

MILADY. Same time tomorrow?

ARAMIS. You bet!

Blackout. Train in tunnel, etc. Lights up. ARAMIS *is even more exhausted.*

MILADY. Good grief.

ARAMIS. I can't breathe.

MILADY. Was all of that legal?

ARAMIS. I wasn't looking.

D'ARTAGNAN (*below window*). Ask her!

ARAMIS. I just need to ask you something.

Blackout. Train in tunnel, etc. Lights up.

MILADY. What a week.

D'ARTAGNAN (*below window*). Now!

MILADY. Is there someone in the garden?

ARAMIS. Do you happen to know where Constance Bonacieux is being held?

MILADY. Constance Bonacieux? You do realise that if I had even the slightest suspicion you were interested in another woman I'd liquidise your head and pour it down the sink.

ARAMIS (*very nervous*). Ha ha ha. Imagine that. Same time tomorrow?

He rushes out and heads downstairs, pulling off the wig as he goes.

That's it. I'm through with this bullsh...

KITTY. Why are you disguised as the Comte de Wardes?

> KITTY *points a gun at him. She's never used a gun and is in an unpredictable state. It could accidentally fire at any moment.*

(*Calling.*) Milady!

ARAMIS. No, Kitty, wait! I can explain.

> *She swings the gun at him.*

You see… the Comte de Wardes is dead.

KITTY. Dead?

ARAMIS. Oh, the mess of it! The tragedy. My closest and dearest friend who I've been obliged to play the double of this past week.

KITTY. What!?

ARAMIS. He got into a duel defending Milady's honour. In his final breath he begged me to step into his shoes! How could I refuse?

KITTY. This is the most screwy thing I've ever heard in my life.

ARAMIS. Which is why it must end tonight.

> *He starts to write on the back of a leaflet left on the table.*

I want you to give her this message from him.

KITTY. What, '*Sorry love, but I'm afraid I'm dead*'!?'

ARAMIS. No. Simply stating that he's ending the relationship.

KITTY. So now she's being dumped by a corpse!? On the back of a sewage-company leaflet?

ARAMIS. Why do you insist on making this sound so unromantic!?

KITTY. You're unbelievable!

ARAMIS (*aside*). All we need now is for the Comte de Wardes to turn up.

> *The* COMTE DE WARDES *turns up.*

COMTE DE WARDES. Hello, Kitty, I'm back! I probably look like the living dead...

KITTY *faints*.

...after such a long journey. Who the heck are you?

ARAMIS *hands him the leaflet*.

ARAMIS. I'm from the sewage company.

...*and then knocks him out with the butt of* KITTY*'s gun*.

MILADY. What's happening down there?

ARAMIS. Nothing. It's just me – Kitty. (*To himself.*) I'm going to kill you, D'Artagnan!

ARAMIS *drags the* COMTE DE WARDES *into the wings. As he turns back,* KITTY *points the gun at him*.

KITTY. What the hell is going on!?

ARAMIS. You hallucinated, Kitty. You thought you saw the Comte but you didn't. And the important thing is this.

KITTY. What?

ARAMIS. I love you.

Blackout. Hallelujah chorus. Lights up.

D'ARTAGNAN. With Kitty!?

ARAMIS. What choice did I have!

D'ARTAGNAN. On top of five nights with Milady de Winter?

ARAMIS. Listen, you don't understand what Milady's like. She a woman who – a woman who – a woman.

D'ARTAGNAN. Well thanks for the penetrating insight. So where's the Comte de Wardes now?

ARAMIS. Tied up in the garden shed.

D'ARTAGNAN. And Milady thinks that – ?

MILADY (*furious, holding a letter*). He's dumping me!?

D'ARTAGNAN. And Kitty thinks that – ?

KITTY. He wants to marry me!

D'ARTAGNAN. You proposed to her!?

ARAMIS. It just popped out!

D'ARTAGNAN. Spare me the details. See you back in Paris cos things are about to get serious.

He sticks on a massive afro wig. He's below MILADY*'s window.*

MILADY. Who are you?

D'ARTAGNAN. Dartington.

MILADY. Dartington who?

D'ARTAGNAN. Tunnel – a friend of the Comte de Wardes. He bitterly regrets his actions and hopes he might be allowed to win back your affections.

MILADY. Well I think we can concoct a suitable reply to that.

D'ARTAGNAN. And we're in.

He rushes upstairs. MILADY*'s room is lit with a candle.*

MILADY. Take off your clothes.

D'ARTAGNAN. Tempting as that *absolutely is* –

He rips off his wig and draws his sword.

My name is D'Artagnan from Gascony, musketeer to King Louis the Thirteenth, defender of the Queen's diamonds and the man you tried to poison in that bar.

MILADY. Well, well, it's the teenager.

D'ARTAGNAN. It was my fellow musketeer Aramis who's been disguised as the Comte de Wardes for the past week. Now tell me where Constance Bonacieux is being held captive or you'll never see the Comte again. Stop laughing!

MILADY. I can't, this is hilarious! All this to find out where Constance Bonacieux is?

D'ARTAGNAN. Tell me!

MILADY. Oh, you really like her, don't you? That's so sweet. But I'm afraid I have no idea where she is.

D'ARTAGNAN. Liar!

She grabs a sword herself.

MILADY. But now? Oh now I'm intrigued.

D'ARTAGNAN. You won't lay a finger on her!

He goes to attack, she blows out the candle. Darkness. Chaos. D'ARTAGNAN *rushes after her into the moonlight. She's gone. He falls to his knees.*

I'm such a fool! Constance, my love, where are you!?

A gun is pointed at his head.

KITTY. And where's my fiancé?

D'ARTAGNAN. Kitty.

A rattling of a door in the wings.

COMTE DE WARDES. My name is the Comte de Wardes. I demand to be released from this tool shed.

As KITTY *is distracted,* D'ARTAGNAN *makes a dash for it. She fires shots after him.*

KITTY. Come back! Where's my fecking fiancé!

Gunshots crossfade into mooing.

Scene Twenty-Five

The CARDINAL *is pacing.* MILADY *enters.*

MILADY. A cowshed? Great secret location – you must be desperate.

CARDINAL RICHELIEU. You're wrong.

MILADY. You're a joke.

CARDINAL RICHELIEU. Okay, let's just ditch the insults and work together, shall we?

MILADY. How's your uprising in La Rochelle working out?

CARDINAL RICHELIEU. It's in my control.

MILADY. Really? I heard you'd underestimated the size of the army Buckingham is currently mobilising in England.

CARDINAL RICHELIEU. The only thing I underestimated was the scale of his obsession with Queen Anne.

MILADY. Bigger than yours you mean?

CARDINAL RICHELIEU. Lord Buckingham needs to be… stopped in his tracks.

MILADY. You want me to give him a dead leg?

CARDINAL RICHELIEU. –

MILADY. You actually want me to kill him? The British Prime Minister? Oh goody. What fun.

CARDINAL RICHELIEU. This is a very serious business.

MILADY. Yes of course it is. Sorry. Serious face.

CARDINAL RICHELIEU. Make it slow. Make it painful. Make him beg for his life.

MILADY. Have you trimmed your goatee?

CARDINAL RICHELIEU. Focus!

MILADY. Okay, I accept the mission, sir! (*Salutes.*) But I want ten thousand.

CARDINAL RICHELIEU. Ten thousand!?

MILADY. I warned you. And I also want one of those 'Get Out of Jail Free' card things.

CARDINAL RICHELIEU. A letter of absolution? Why?

MILADY. Because I'll need something to get me off the hook if I get caught, durr.

CARDINAL RICHELIEU. But you won't get caught.

MILADY. So write it. And I also want /

CARDINAL RICHELIEU. Oh here we go. What is it this time? Dolphin-skin slippers? A zebra salad?

MILADY. You're so odd. I want to know where Constance is being held.

CARDINAL RICHELIEU. Interesting. Why?

MILADY. Call it retribution.

CARDINAL RICHELIEU. This wouldn't have anything to do with the musketeer D'Artagnan, would it? What's he done to ruffle your feathers?

MILADY. It doesn't need to concern you.

CARDINAL RICHELIEU. Well I'm not going to let you harm the Queen's lady-in-waiting. It would cause me too many problems.

MILADY. Then the whole deal's off.

CARDINAL RICHELIEU. But I'm very happy to do something about the musketeer.

MILADY. Very well. I deal with Buckingham, you eliminate D'Artagnan and we're even.

CARDINAL RICHELIEU. Gladly.

MILADY. The letter.

He signs and hands her the letter of absolution.

CARDINAL RICHELIEU. Be careful.

MILADY. So sweet.

She kisses him and exits.

Scene Twenty-Six

She turns a corner into wind and rain. She is grabbed by ATHOS *and thrown to the floor. The scene is melodramatic, taking place on a clifftop.*

MILADY. Who the hell are you?

ATHOS. I wouldn't believe it at first. But it just kept niggling away at me – the possibility that you might still be alive. And I knew that if I kept track of the Cardinal, sooner or later I'd discover the truth.

ATHOS *removes his hat.*

How did you do it?

MILADY. Well, well. The last time I saw you, I was sat on a horse under a tree with a rope around my neck.

ATHOS. I should have stayed. And saved the world from having you in it any longer.

MILADY. Bit harsh. Considering it was you who made me into what I am!

ATHOS. Of course. It was never you, was it? All I ever did was love you.

MILADY. I was so young. I could've changed.

ATHOS. You had no intention of changing.

ATHOS *draws his sword.*

MILADY. Oh hello. Here's an example of a man who thinks he can kill me… but he can't. That's why he chose a horse to do it on his behalf, isn't it. And ever since then he's had trouble sleeping. Am I right? Have you actually managed to be with another woman since that day?

ATHOS. You have a black heart.

MILADY. Put down the sword, Athos.

ATHOS. I heard everything that passed between you and the Cardinal.

MILADY. Lucky you. So neither of us knows where your friend D'Artagnan's little girlfriend is.

ATHOS. Hand over that letter of absolution. No one's going to be killing Lord Buckingham on my watch. Let it go.

MILADY. I can't. I don't know how to be anything else. Kill me.

ATHOS. The letter.

As she hands him the letter, she drops it and plunges a knife into his outstretched hand and escapes, taking the letter. Ribbon-blood spurts from ATHOS*'s hand.*

Why did I have to love her so much!?

Scene Twenty-Seven

D'ARTAGNAN *sits at a bar alone, desperate. The* PUB
LANDLORD *pours him a glass of wine.*

PUB LANDLORD. Never run back to what you broke, that's
what I say.

D'ARTAGNAN. Excuse me?

PUB LANDLORD. If life gives you lemons, make lemonade.

D'ARTAGNAN. Right.

PUB LANDLORD. No one's as deaf as the man who won't
listen.

D'ARTAGNAN. No, I'm totally prepared to listen /

PUB LANDLORD. But *are* you? Strangers are just friends you
haven't met.

D'ARTAGNAN. Yeah, I'm not really sure any of these apply to
my situation, actually.

PUB LANDLORD. Drink your wine, it'll help.

He's about to drink when ATHOS *enters on his bike.*

ATHOS. No!

D'ARTAGNAN. Athos, at last. Where have you been?

ATHOS. Don't drink that, there's a price on your head. He's
probably poisoned it.

D'ARTAGNAN. Don't be ridiculous.

PUB LANDLORD. Yeah, don't be ridiculous, I'm just one of
those regular old pub landlords, full of wise advice.

ATHOS. Step away from the bar, Cushion-Face! Regular
landlord, eh? You're not even wearing trousers. Drink
the wine.

D'ARTAGNAN. Athos, there might be a simpler explanation /

ATHOS. Drink it before I run you through!

PUB LANDLORD *drinks the wine.*

D'ARTAGNAN. I'm really sorry about my friend, mate.

PUB LANDLORD *begins to choke and collapses*.

Or maybe I'm not.

ATHOS. Looks like someone's gonna be waking up with a bit more than a hangover.

D'ARTAGNAN. I don't think he's gonna be waking up at all.

ATHOS. Yeah, that's actually what I meant.

D'ARTAGNAN. Who's trying to kill me? Milady de Winter?

ATHOS. You mean my ex-wife?

D'ARTAGNAN. Milady de Winter's your…

ATHOS. I just refused to believe she might still be alive. (*Reacts to his stabbed hand*.)

D'ARTAGNAN. So you met her?

ATHOS *goes behind the bar and mixes cocktails for the two of them*.

ATHOS. Let's say we had an exchange of words. I overheard her making a pact with the Cardinal. He agreed to kill you in return for her assassinating Lord Buckingham.

D'ARTAGNAN. Buckingham? But what about Constance?

ATHOS. Constance is safe. The Cardinal refused to divulge her wherabouts.

D'ARTAGNAN. But *he* knows. I'll kill him.

ATHOS. No. Leave the investigation of that to me. The Queen has requested you go to England to warn Lord Buckingham. Take my horse.

D'ARTAGNAN. Really?

ATHOS. Just watch out when you're in gallop mode – her chain can come loose.

D'ARTAGNAN. So where are Aramis and Porthos?

ATHOS. Called up by the King himself to fight the rebels in La Rochelle – those Protestants are really kicking off and Buckingham's raising an army to come and support them.

D'ARTAGNAN. Hang on, I'm going to England to save Buckingham's life, right?

ATHOS. Yeah, I know where you're going with this.

D'ARTAGNAN. So in doing our duty to the Queen by saving Lord Buckingham, we're actively supporting the Protestant uprising we're fighting against?

ATHOS. Did any war ever make any sense?

D'ARTAGNAN. I guess not.

They down the cocktails ATHOS *has poured.*

ATHOS. Go.

Scene Twenty-Eight

D'ARTAGNAN *sets off. Split-image. We also see* MILADY *travelling to England.* D'ARTAGNAN *arrives first and reaches* BUCKINGHAM, *who listens and then sends out orders. We then see* MILADY *being arrested (witnessed by* D'ARTAGNAN) *and brought before* BUCKINGHAM.

BUCKINGHAM. What are we today? Russian? South American perhaps?

MILADY. Vous êtes un twat pompeux – as we say in France.

BUCKINGHAM. And you're nicked – as we say here in England.

MILADY. For what, Lord Buckingham?

BUCKINGHAM. You're denying you came here to kill me?

MILADY. I just came for a little holiday.

BUCKINGHAM. That was a neat little trick you pulled in my woodshed.

MILADY. I certainly remember pulling something little.

BUCKINGHAM. I was impressed.

MILADY. I wasn't.

BUCKINGHAM. How am I going to keep you out of trouble while I'm invading your country?

MILADY. Well I wouldn't lock me up.

BUCKINGHAM. And why is that?

MILADY. I'll escape.

BUCKINGHAM. You've obviously never been to an English jail.

She is moved to a cell by a guard. Action.

You will be a resident of His Majesty's highest security jail in Shepton Mallet.

MILADY. Sorry, hang on…

Music pauses for…

Did you say Shepton Mallet?

BUCKINGHAM. Don't be fooled – the walls are fifteen-feet thick, sixty-foot high and the interlocking door system is the most advanced in Europe. You will be under twenty-four-hour watch, led by the most ruthless and unyielding man in my army – Lieutenant John Felton. Code name: The Rock.

She is thrown onto the lowest platform – her cell. FELTON steps forward.

Scene Twenty-Nine

MILADY. Why do they call you The Rock? Is it because you're emotionally impenetrable? Or because you've got a face like a bag of gravel?

FELTON. Lights out.

Blackout. Lights fade up with dawn. (FELTON *is in a new position each time lights fade up*.)

MILADY. Come on, Rock, it's been two days now and not a peep out of you. Fine – 'cold reading' it is then.

Blackout. The lights fade up.

So. We've established that you're not married, you hated your father, you want to tell your mother you love her before she dies and despite saving Lord Buckingham's life *three times* he's always overlooked you for promotion. Anything to add?

FELTON. Lights out.

Blackout. The lights fade up.

MILADY. I spent most of my childhood hiding from my father. I'd lie in cornfields listening to the earth. I had so many dreams for the future. What's your dream? Come on – what is it you've always dreamt of doing?

A butterfly appears. It captures FELTON*'s attention.* MILADY *notices.*

There *is* something – something you've never let on to anyone. Come on, Johnny, tell me.

The butterfly lands near MILADY.

My goodness, what are you doing here, you little beauty? The future isn't looking good for you, is it.

FELTON. Don't kill it! (*Butterflies are his secret passion.*)

MILADY. Why not?

FELTON. It's a Queen of Spain fritillary – incredibly rare to the British Isle!

MILADY. You're mistaken. It's a Danaus plexippus and this little lady – no black spots on her hindwings – is even rarer than your Issoria lathonia. She must have been caught in a headwind on her migration from Canada to Mexico. She must be starving.

FELTON. I didn't know you...

MILADY. No, well you didn't ask, did you, Mr Chatty-Man. Don't just stand there, she needs milkweed!

FELTON (*panicked*). There's no milkweed in Shepton Mallet!

MILADY. So lilac, Buddleja, sedum.

FELTON. There's a tray of oregano in the kitchen.

MILADY. That'll do. Hurry!

He departs.

(*Calling after him.*) Because when she puts the call out to her fellow travellers, we'll be inundated.

FELTON *returns,* MILADY *is surrounded by butterflies.*

You won't see a sight like this ever again in your life! Oregano now!

FELTON *enters the cell and holds out the tray of oregano. Butterflies swarm around them.*

The Mexicans believe they carry the souls of their ancestors. Every year, one hundred million of them make a four-thousand-mile journey and no one knows why. It's one of the most incredible migrations in the natural world.

FELTON. I've always dreamt of running a butterfly farm!

MILADY. Me too. Oh let's do it, John Felton, you beautiful rock of a man! Let's establish the world's first butterfly farm!

They hold hands and jump out of the prison. The butterflies fly off. FELTON *comes to his senses.*

Scene Thirty

FELTON. What am I doing? You're a convicted criminal.

MILADY. John, listen to me. Men have wronged me all my life – for the crime of being different. They've felt justified in doing terrible things to me. And the worst one of them all? Lord Buckingham. You saved his life three times. And for what?

FELTON. People like him never see nor care what happens to those below them – the people who are expected to die like cattle in their feckless wars.

MILADY. Exactly! And he'll destroy our dream too unless we destroy him first?

FELTON *produces a knife. He cuts his palm then grabs* MILADY's *palm and does the same before slapping them together.*

FELTON. The bastard won't see the morning light.

MILADY. I'll be waiting in Plymouth, beside the next boat to Spain.

FELTON. Spain?

MILADY. Best place for butterflies. And eloping. Hurry!

He exits.

(*To audience.*) Oops.

BUCKINGHAM *stands on a platform holding a scroll that reads 'La Rochelle Battle Plans'.* FELTON *climbs up behind him, stabs him and exits. Ribbon-blood spurts out of* BUCKINGHAM's *stomach.*

BERTIE (*off*). Georgie, a letter has arrived for you from France.

BERTIE (BUCKINGHAM's *friend*) *enters.*

Georgie, no! Who did this?

BUCKINGHAM. Bertie, my friend, I am done for. Tell Queen Anne that I loved her more than I ever thought it possible to love someone.

BERTIE. I came here with a letter from her.

BUCKINGHAM. Read it for me. There's blood in my eyes.

BERTIE. 'Dear Georgie, my English muffin, even though we can't be together, I want you to know that I love you. Signed, your Anne.

BUCKINGHAM. Then I die content in that knowledge at least.

BERTIE. I vow to you, Georgie, that I will dedicate every day of my life, I will mobilise every soldier, every horse, every zeppelin in order to discover who was responsible for this!

BUCKINGHAM. It was John Felton.

BERTIE. Oh. Right. Then John Felton shall pay the price!

'Plymouth Docks'. FELTON looks frantically for MILADY. *Then he sees her – on board a 'boat to France'.*

FELTON. What are you doing, you said you'd wait. You said we were going to Spain. What about the butterflies!?

MILADY. I fucking hate butterflies, John Felton. My father was a lepidopterist and the cruellest man I've ever known.

BERTIE *enters and points a musket at* FELTON*'s head.*

BERTIE. I'm arresting you for the murder of Lord Buckingham.

FELTON. No, *she's* the one you should be arresting! On that boat to France. That's Milady de Winter!

BERTIE *looks up in horror. Sound effect: thunder and lightning, plus music, transitions us to France, but* MILADY *remains in her position. The cast help transition the actor playing* BERTIE (EMMA) *into* CARDINAL RICHELIEU.

Scene Thirty-One

MILADY (*furious*). Cardinal Richelieu. Cardinal Richelieu.

He appears.

CARDINAL RICHELIEU. Will you keep your voice down!

MILADY. Why is D'Artagnan still alive? We had a deal.

CARDINAL RICHELIEU. Forget D'Artagnan. He and his three friends are national heroes. They practically crushed the Protestant uprising in La Rochelle quadruple-handedly.

MILADY. So that plan of yours to keep them under control kind of backfired then, didn't it? Very well, give me the address of Constance Bonacieux instead.

CARDINAL RICHELIEU. No way.

MILADY. You have no choice.

CARDINAL RICHELIEU. What are you talking about?

MILADY. When John Felton stands trial for Lord Buckingham's murder, he will say that I talked him into it. And when they come looking for me I shall simply point the finger at you.

CARDINAL RICHELIEU. You honestly think that anyone will take the word of a criminal above the most powerful man in France?

MILADY. They will when they see the letter absolving me of Buckingham's murder. Signed by you.

CARDINAL RICHELIEU. Oh crap.

MILADY. Now, if you want it back, tell me the address.

CARDINAL RICHELIEU. The Carmelite Convent at Bethune.

MILADY. A convent? You're lying.

CARDINAL RICHELIEU. She believes she was placed there by the Queen to keep her safe.

MILADY. So she wouldn't try to escape? Oh clever little Cardinal.

CARDINAL RICHELIEU. But you won't get in. They're a strict order who never accept newcomers.

MILADY. Please. You think I can't get into a flipping convent?

CARDINAL RICHELIEU. The letter.

MILADY. I think I should keep it. Just in case. Don't you?

She exits.

CARDINAL RICHELIEU. Oh Lord forgive me, what have I done? Why doesn't anything ever go right for me!? Those damn musketeers! I am not prevailing.

Scene Thirty-Two

Battlements in La Rochelle. Sound effect: crowd.

VOICES. Speech, speech, speech, speech.

ATHOS. Friends, soldiers, citizens of La Rochelle, people of France. This is your victory. Your unbending resolve was never weakened and I salute you. This is also a day of reckoning that should send a message loud and clear throughout France; that the King's musketeers must be reinstated!

Cheers.

D'ARTAGNAN. Great speech, Athos.

ATHOS. Only made possible by the fact that you saved my life on the battlement.

D'ARTAGNAN. Then we're even.

ATHOS. We are. And I need a drink!

He exits. ARAMIS *enters hurriedly with a letter.*

ARAMIS. D'Artagnan, It's a message from Cardinal Richelieu; it's the address of where Constance Bonacieux is being held.

D'ARTAGNAN. Why is he suddenly giving it to us?

ARAMIS. I've no idea. But something tells me we don't have a moment to lose. Come on!

Scene Thirty-Three

'The Carmelite Convent at Bethune'. MILADY (*in disguise as a nun), knocks.* SISTER MARY *opens a shutter.*

SISTER MARY. How can I help you?

MILADY (*lost*). The answer is Jesus, what is the question?

SISTER MARY. Excuse me?

MILADY. Have you ever thought about accepting the Lord into your life?

SISTER MARY. You do realise this is a convent?

MILADY. What? Oh no. I've been doing this so long, I don't even recognise the institution where my journey once began.

SISTER MARY. Doing what for so long, my child?

MILADY. Going door to door, across France, spreading the word of God.

SISTER MARY. How long have you been doing this?

MILADY. Months? Possibly years, surviving on scraps, sleeping in doorways.

SISTER MARY. Oh my poor girl, you must come in and let us help you.

MILADY *enters and the door closes.*

Just wait here a moment.

SISTER MARY *exits.* MILADY *removes her tattered habit and heads into the building.* SISTER MARY *returns.*

Where did she go? (*Sees the door ajar.*) She must have run off. Oh, the poor creature.

Meanwhile, MILADY *passes another* NUN, *praying with her back to us.* MILADY *grabs a pot of flowers.*

MILADY. Fresh flowers for Madame Bonacieux. Which is her room?

The NUN *points.*

Thanks. Vow of silence? How long have you managed?

NUN. Five years. You cow!

MILADY *enters a room.* CONSTANCE *turns from looking out of the window*

MILADY. Fresh flowers.

CONSTANCE. Hello. I haven't seen you before.

MILADY (*feigning danger*). Shhh. Constance, I need you to listen to me very carefully.

CONSTANCE. Who are you?

MILADY. A friend of D'Artagnan. He's instructed me to take you to a safe house. But we must hurry.

CONSTANCE. But I've just received word that he's coming for me himself.

MILADY. Have you?

CONSTANCE. Yes.

MILADY (*aside*). Interesting. (*To* CONSTANCE.) Well there's been a change of plan because he's still detained in La Rochelle, fighting the Protestants. And you're in great danger.

CONSTANCE. Who from? What's going on?

MILADY. The Cardinal's guards are heading here as we speak to take you away.

CONSTANCE. Why?

MILADY. Did D'Artagnan tell you nothing of the Cardinal's plot to assassinate the King?

CONSTANCE. Assassinate the King!?

MILADY. And the only person who'll stop him is D'Artagnan. So the Cardinal's plan is to capture you and use you as bait – to lure D'Artagnan in and kill him.

CONSTANCE. Oh God.

MILADY. You'll be safe in my château though. It's remote, secluded. We'll be waiting for D'Artagnan there.

CONSTANCE. I'm not sure about this.

MILADY. Constance, the Cardinal's guards could be here any moment!

Sound effect: horses approaching.

That'll be them now.

CONSTANCE. It might be D'Artagnan.

She rushes to the window.

MILADY. And if it's not? We must hurry! What on earth are you doing now!?

CONSTANCE. Having a panic attack!

MILADY. There's no time for a flipping panic attack! (*Sotto.*) Right, plan B. (*To* CONSTANCE.) Here, drink this.

She pours a glass of water, into which she pours a powder.

Drink it, it'll calm you down.

CONSTANCE *does and immediately starts to choke.*

Bye, bye, Constance.

She rushes out of the room, only to meet D'ARTAGNAN *coming the other way.*

D'ARTAGNAN. Where is she?

There is a ferocious Apache fight, during which SISTER MARY *rushes to* CONSTANCE *and tries to revive her.* D'ARTAGNAN *badly wounds* MILADY *and then rushes to* CONSTANCE *himself.*

Constance, no, stay with me. I love you. I'd sacrifice the world for you. You are happiness to me. You breathed on me and made my life a richer one to live.

CONSTANCE *dies*.

No!

SISTER MARY. I'm so sorry.

MILADY *has made it up the stairs. She points a gun.*

MILADY. And I thought it was you and I who'd be the great romance. Goodbye, D'Artagnan.

SISTER MARY *pulls out a gun and shoots* MILADY *dead*.

SISTER MARY. This is a house of God!

CONSTANCE *gasps air then sits up and gets to her feet*.

AL (*sotto*). Emma, what are you doing? You're dead.

EMMA. No. We can't do this any more.

AL. Can't do what any more?

EMMA. There's enough tragedy in the world without Constance dying as well.

AL. What are you talking about? It's in the book.

EMMA. I don't care about the book! These people haven't spent thirty-five pounds a ticket to see something this upsetting.

AL. Nineteen actually.

EMMA. It doesn't matter how much they paid. What matters is that… nineteen pounds? Seriously?

AL. It's great value.

EMMA. What matters is that we send people home with a sense of optimism. Hope. Tragedy's easy. We need a bit more effort going into making people happy, don't you think?

DAN. That deserves to go on a tea towel, Emma. And framed.

They high-five.

AL. Okay. Let's do this then.

MILADY. So does that mean that I /

DAN. No.

He shoots MILADY.

D'ARTAGNAN. Constance.

CONSTANCE. D'Artagnan.

*They embrace to swelling music and start to exit together.
But there's no time to be alone because* D'ARTAGNAN'*s
ceremony is about to begin. Trumpets sound.* CONSTANCE
ushers D'ARTAGNAN *back and exits.*

Scene Thirty-Four

KING LOUIS. Well now, D'Artagnan, you and your three
friends are quite the talk of France. The throne may well
have toppled without your help.

D'ARTAGNAN. I'm just pleased I had the opportunity to serve
you, Your Majesty.

KING LOUIS. That's the spirit. Think you could beat me in
a sword fight?

D'ARTAGNAN. I wouldn't like to speculate.

KING LOUIS. Come on, speculate – could you beat me in
a sword fight?

D'ARTAGNAN. Yes.

KING LOUIS. Show-off. Are your parents here for the
ceremony?

D'ARTAGNAN. They're somewhere out there in the crowd.

KING LOUIS. Where's my wife got to?

QUEEN ANNE. Here.

KING LOUIS. That's a relief.

QUEEN ANNE. D'Artagnan, beyond my gratitude, I wish to offer you my congratulations.

D'ARTAGNAN. Thank you. I'm very sorry to hear about Lord Buckingham.

KING LOUIS. I'm not. The pompous little Etonian.

QUEEN ANNE. Thank you. And how is Constance?

D'ARTAGNAN. She's back on her feet. Doing well.

QUEEN ANNE. That shipping accident her husband died in was rather unfortunate.

D'ARTAGNAN. Yes.

QUEEN ANNE. Well, on to business. The public outcry for the reinstatement of the King's musketeers was overwhelming. Great shame your friends aren't here to witness this actually.

D'ARTAGNAN. Yeah they're... busy.

QUEEN ANNE. And the Cardinal's over the moon too. Aren't you.

CARDINAL RICHELIEU. Yes, Your Majesty.

QUEEN ANNE. He's not. He's seething. And Lord only knows what he's been up to recently. But we shall probably never find out because he's the Cardinal. And we can't get rid of him. Now then, can we have some trumpets please? And you'll need to kneel, D'Artagnan.

Trumpets sound. Lights change for ceremony. She hands D'ARTAGNAN *a musketeer's costume.*

D'Artagnan of Gascony, in the year of our lord, 1625, I salute you as an official King's musketeer. And to this grand and proud country that my husband and I are *temporarily* custodians of, to this tiny speck of a tiny speck in an unimaginably large universe, I say that I am absolutely opposed to those who say France for the French and let our neighbours go hang. If I do not call myself a patriot, it does not alter the fact that I have an intense pride for being the

French Queen and I will not consent to seeing our nation stifled by outmoded ideals of sovereignty. We are a world people, we belong to the world, and that is the message my King's musketeers will embody!

Sound effect: cheers.

KING LOUIS. Whatever she said. Right. Who's for tea and cakes?

Scene Thirty-Five

Ceremony dissolves away. D'ARTAGNAN *is left alone, looking out.*

Then he starts to get changed. He runs back down towards the den and joins the others who are also changing into new musketeers' costumes.

D'ARTAGNAN. Guys, come on, hurry up!

ARAMIS. All right, all right, hang on.

PORTHOS. Where are we going?

D'ARTAGNAN. Dunno.

ATHOS. Oh wow. Wow! These are *such* cool uniforms!

PORTHOS. These are like, *really* cool. Your mum is an absolute flipping legend, mate.

ARAMIS. She really made them all herself?

D'ARTAGNAN. Yep. She's kind of the best mum in the world. And she also got us these.

ARAMIS. No way.

ATHOS. You. Are. Kidding.

ARAMIS. Proper swords!?

PORTHOS. What!?

ATHOS. THIS IS AWESOMMMMME!!

ARAMIS. How does it feel to officially be a King's musketeer, D'Artagnan?

D'ARTAGNAN. It feels… really, really happy.

ATHOS. Gentlemen… and ladies.

BECKY. Thank you.

ATHOS. Mount your steeds.

They get on their bikes.

ARAMIS. So. Where to?

ATHOS. I say we head south.

ARAMIS. Why?

ATHOS. Just… cos I say so.

PORTHOS. Yeah but you're not the leader.

ATHOS. Well I'm eleven, so I kind of am.

ARAMIS. There are no leaders, Athos. We're a partnership.

D'ARTAGNAN. Yeah, we're a partnership. Of musketeers. And we have missions to complete, people to save and a whole summer to fill.

ATHOS. A damn fine speech, D'Artagnan! Dignified, perfectly punctuated, I love you more than… okay who put coke in my grape juice again?

OTHERS. All for one and one for all!

ELO's 'Mr. Blue Sky' kicks in. They ride off in a joyful world of their own.

End.

Other Adaptations in this Series

ANIMAL FARM
Ian Wooldridge
Adapted from George Orwell

ANNA KARENINA
Helen Edmundson
Adapted from Leo Tolstoy

ARABIAN NIGHTS
Dominic Cooke

AROUND THE WORLD IN 80 DAYS
Laura Eason
Adapted from Jules Verne

THE CANTERBURY TALES
Mike Poulton
Adapted from Geoffrey Chaucer

A CHRISTMAS CAROL
Karen Louise Hebden
Adapted from Charles Dickens

CORAM BOY
Helen Edmundson
Adapted from Jamila Gavin

DAVID COPPERFIELD
Alastair Cording
Adapted from Charles Dickens

DIARY OF A NOBODY
Hugh Osborne
Adapted from George Grossmith
& Wheedon Grossmith

DR JEKYLL AND MR HYDE
David Edgar
Adapted from Robert Louis Stevenson

DRACULA: THE BLOODY TRUTH
Le Navet Bete & John Nicholson
Adapted from Bram Stoker

EMMA
Martin Millar and Doon MacKichan
Adapted from Jane Austen

FRANKENSTEIN
Patrick Sandford
Adapted from Mary Shelley

GREAT EXPECTATIONS
Nick Ormerod and Declan Donnellan
Adapted from Charles Dickens

THE HAUNTING
Hugh Janes
Adapted from Charles Dickens

HIS DARK MATERIALS
Nicholas Wright
Adapted from Philip Pullman

THE HOUND OF
THE BASKERVILLES
Steven Canny & John Nicholson
Adapted from Arthur Conan Doyle

JANE EYRE
Polly Teale
Adapted from Charlotte Brontë

JEEVES AND WOOSTER IN
PERFECT NONSENSE
The Goodale Brothers
Adapted from P.G. Wodehouse

THE JUNGLE BOOK
Stuart Paterson
Adapted from Rudyard Kipling

KENSUKE'S KINGDOM
Stuart Paterson
Adapted from Michael Morpurgo

KES
Lawrence Till
Adapted from Barry Hines

THE MASSIVE TRAGEDY
OF MADAME BOVARY
John Nicholson & Javier Marzan
Adapted from Gustave Flaubert

NOUGHTS & CROSSES
Dominic Cooke
Adapted from Malorie Blackman

THE RAGGED TROUSERED
PHILANTHROPISTS
Howard Brenton
Adapted from Robert Tressell

THE RAILWAY CHILDREN
Mike Kenny
Adapted from E. Nesbit

SWALLOWS AND AMAZONS
Helen Edmundson and Neil Hannon
Adapted from Arthur Ransome

TREASURE ISLAND
Stuart Paterson
Adapted from Robert Louis Stevenson

THE WIND IN THE WILLOWS
Mike Kenny
Adapted from Kenneth Grahame